It's Worth It: How to Talk To Your Right-Wing Relatives, Friends, and Neighbors

This page intentionally left blank

Copyright & Contact

Email: egberto@egbertowillies.com
Web: http://egbertowillies.com
Twitter: http://twitter.com/egbertowillies

Table of Contents

Chapter 1: Introduction

I read a lot of news websites, blogs, and online journals. I do not get a chance to read a lot of books anymore as activist journalism is in the moment and very time consuming.

I wish all the great authors out there would make two versions of their books, a condensed version and the one where the fluff is there to make the book more enjoyable and human. For those of us who want to get to the point and move on it would be helpful.

This book is the condensed version. So far, I have completed two books; "As I See It: Class Warfare The Only Resort To Right Wing Doom," (ISBN-13: 978-1453608166), a 205 page book, and "Lose Weight And Be Fit Now," a 50 page book. The latter is very matter of fact and to the point. The former is a bit more expansive.

I have several others already in progress based mostly on my activism and policy. Most are likely to be condensed versions where nothing is lost in their brevity. After-all, Timothy Snyder got a whole lot of information in 128 pages in his book "On Tyranny," a must read.

The one thing I promise with all my books is honesty along with objective clear eyedness. Most importantly, as a fallible human being, I promise the humility necessary to adjust when things change or if for any reason it is proven that I have taken an invalid path.

Let us get busy talking to our Right-Wing brothers and sisters. It is not hard once you remember that positive communication is not only a benefit for "them" but for "us" as well.

I start by telling a small bit of my story so one understands what may have been injected in my analytical framing. I feel that gives one the ability to color one's word with the proper context.

I then go into what my experience has shown me to frame many on the Right. There are many Ph.Ds. that have studied this, and many books written. My perspective is a continuum.

Chapter 6: Informational Essays, contains several modified articles I have written for various publications. Their intent is to bolster our Progressive framing on several issues so that as you encounter conversations specifically on the right one can be sufficiently grounded in our core beliefs. Many times, while we know what we stand for, the words do not always flow out.

My blogs, internet programs, and my radio/media program Politics Done Right gives me the unique opportunity to interact with dozens if not hundreds of people of all stripes on a weekly basis. Ironically, I have a lot of listeners, viewers, and readers from the Right. Many of them interact with our programs and blogs daily.

Chapter 2: My Story

When writing on a subject about talking and trying to reach the most profound feelings and beliefs of others it is important that one also understand the life experiences of the writer. It is important because much will be refracted through those lenses.

The impression most coming from Central America, the Caribbean, and South America is that one is coming to an advance country where most are very smart. It is assumed that the people of the country are logical, and that the United States' success can be attributed to its logic and purported level of education.

The election of Donald Trump turns that on its head. The United States' mistake has lost us the respect. Whereas we were considered the backstop, the bastion of stability, that has all evaporated.

Our dysfunctional government has made us a national disgrace. It is ironic that while Donald Trump has been trying to close our borders, in the long run, it is the borders of the rest of the world that is closed to us as the advent of our dismal response to COVID-19 has made us persona non grata in virtually every country around the world.

There is a symbiotic relationship between failed government and apathy. And apathy comes about when everyone feels impotent.

Recovery from said impotence requires that we solve our polarization problem. That can only be accomplished with dialogue, one that those in power would prefer we not have. You see, in this chaos they profit.

Coming to America

I left Tocumen airport in Panama and landed in the big city of Houston on my way to Blinn College in Brenham Texas. That was the genesis to developing my communication skills in a place/people-dependent manner. And it occurred less than an hour into my arrival in America.

It was 1979. This green-behind-the-ear teenager went into the Greyhound bus station completely lost. I went to the counter and had the following encounter. To be clear, it was scary for a newcomer knowing little about the country. It has been a few decades, but this is the dialogue as I remember it.

I am from the Atlantic side of Panama, the Province of Colon. The Panamanians there have heavy Caribbean roots. We speak English with more of a Caribbean twang and Spanish with the distinctive Panamanian tone. In other word I had a strong accent.

"Good evening," I said to the lady at the Greyhound counter.

I recall she just looked at me. In other words, I recall her being very rude even before she spoke a word. It was 1979.

"May I get a bus ticket to BREN-HAM Texas?" I asked.

"There is no BREN-HAM Texas," she snapped.

By now I am in a panic. Did I land at the right airport? Did I get the wrong college? Hell, I did not know.

I went into my briefcase. Yes, I was prepared for the new country with a cheap briefcase as well. I took out the book/brochure from Blinn College and asked her how to get to BREN-HAM Texas.

"That is not BREN-HAM Texas," she snapped again. "That is BREN-UM Texas."

"Mam," I said very respectfully. "Can I get a ticket to BREN-UM Texas?"

"That will be $40.00," she said or something like that.

I arrived in Brenham, Texas, excited to get started. Brenham was neither cosmopolitan nor vibrant. It was not the America I expected.

I was a wet behind-the-ears black kid that spoke with an accent in a country town. The African American kids were suspicious of me, the white American kids were curious, and the Latino American kids giggled when I spoke to them in

Spanish. I hung out with Peruvian, Argentinian, Guatemalan, and Venezuelan friends most of that year.

We were all strangers in a new land away from our parents for the first time who shared one thing in common — we could all communicate in Spanish and when strange things happened, we could enter our cocoon. It is amazing how quickly and quietly human beings adapt.

America revealed

We were walking down one of the few commercial streets in Brenham when some guys in a pickup truck just started shouting nigger and, if I remember correctly, something about being in the wrong part of town. It was directed solely at me because, while we were all Latinos walking down that street, I was the only black one.

I remember going to Padre Island for spring break, six of us packed like sardines in my car. I remember getting to the beach house and the coldness with which I was treated on the island, compared to my geographic brothers and sisters from South and Central America. Funny thing is they never had a clue.

I always knew Blinn was a steppingstone to move up, and I moved up to The University of Texas at Austin (UT) after a year at Blinn. I had no problem getting in on my own merit, but most of my friends assumed I got in thanks to some quota (they did not realize as a foreigner I did not qualify). Both students and professors in many instances went out of their way to remind me that I was an "other." I rallied the campus for UT's divestiture from South Africa given their overtly brutal apartheid system. I understood that fighting injustices somewhere else helped to hold up a mirror to the injustices we faced locally.

I remember being stopped many times by the police. It is not that I was a bad driver. Most of the stops seemed to have only to do with a desire to question me. It was never confrontational. I did as I was told. You see, where I am from, Panama, a dispute with an officer guarantees a cracked skull with no legal recourse, so the cops in Austin likely thought I was a model citizen. From a young age, I always knew when and where to engage. I adapted.

When I graduated from UT and went to work, I encountered the same preconceived notions. But work is not the cops. I was vocal and never took any crap. Suffice it to say I had 5 jobs in 5 years and finally formed my own software company. When my company became successful, I moved to Kingwood, a nice suburb with a lot of trees and a particularly good school system for my daughter.

My first memorable experience in Kingwood was walking in the trails and passing a white woman who immediately held her purse tightly and looked at me with horror. I looked at her and simply shook my head, seething. Another time I went cycling with one of my new friends and stopped in at a convenience store. When we left the store my friend simply said, "I get it now." I guess I was his first black friend. Inside that store, he saw how differently a person with my skin color is treated.

How one ultimately resolves their interaction with others is generally predicated by past experiences. Some either decide to always stay in a place of comfort. Others explore. I explore.

My parents instilled in all their kids that they were just as good and no better than anyone irrespective of their socio-economic-ethnic-racial background. And that was important in who I became. It meant that I never feared engaging.

What I never learned at home was how to strategically back down or reframe my words for more effective communication. That is only true where the police are not involved. Because of my origin, we have a necessary "respect" for the police. Ironically in America, the bastion of freedom, respect or disrespect of the police does not guarantee People of Color a positive outcome in an encounter with the police.

At the University of Texas, I was combative with professors who I knew were judging me by different standards. On my different places of employment, because I knew too many believe I was a "quota" hire, I made my competency known in no uncertain terms. And anytime I felt, aggrieved, I simply quit and moved on, five jobs in five years.

As I got older, I realized that if I dropped the chip off my shoulder, I was likely a quota hire.

Competence and being hired to fulfill a quota is not mutually exclusive That in itself proved the necessity for Affirmative Action since there is a more than 50% likelihood, my competence would not be enough to get many jobs I was qualified for given my hue. Lived experience is probative.

Lowering of the guard

For an exceedingly long time, I had my guard up and was ready to charge anyone who challenged me on terms I thought were meant to demean who I was, challenge my intelligence, or challenge whether I belonged. My mechanism came from having been judged and stereotyped because I was foreign and because I was black.

This is the same mechanism for Right-Wingers, Left-Wingers, and anyone who feels aggrieved whether real, imagined, or implanted. To get out of that mode one needs a catalyst to jar a change in behavior, a change in communication.

My jarring came in two distinct phases. And they were more than a decade apart.

On my way to China I got into a discussion with my then business partner about homosexuality.

It was the late nineties on a trip to China with my then business partner, Joe. I cannot remember why I was ranting against gays. You see, I am tricultural, black, Caribbean, Latino, and each of these subcultures has strong homophobic streaks.

"Can you change your race?" Joe asked paraphrased.

"No," I answered. "Nor would I want to do so."

"A gay person could live an easy nonconfrontational life by denying who they are," Joe said then, again paraphrased.

As simple as that exchange was, it went off like a bright light bulb in my head. Though not cured, from the heart, the brain was reeducated and rewired in that instant.

Change from the heart took much longer. I knew my homophobia was cured not only from the mind but equally from the heart when I had no negative gut reaction in the presence of my gay brothers and sisters doing what heterosexuals do.

It was a feeling of personal accomplishment. You see, it was my problem, my failure. I went from being a homophobe to a huge gay rights supporter, a part of my atonement.

Culture and how one was reared is not easy to overcome. Even when one makes the intellectual transition, "muscle memory" many times continue to lurk. It takes a lot of work to change "muscle memory" permanently.

My second phase of change came during the 2009 Affordable Care Act debate. It seemed like the country was busting from the seams. Each side could not believe how evil the other side was.

The thing is those with egalitarian thoughts were right for the policies they wanted. Those with patriarchal or Ayn Randian belief-sets were correct for the policies they supported or the lack thereof.

Because of this chasm, communication between poles was impossible. It was then that I saw a video by a young woman with a group called the Coffee Party USA. The goal of the group was just to get people of all viewpoints to have a nonjudgmental seat and have a cup of coffee.

Watching the pain in the woman's eyes and voice pleading for civility touched me. I joined the group early on and to this day remain on the board of directors.

We promote civil discourse. The expectation is that ultimately consensus can be reached on issues but at worse, living with the democratically winning solution.

Working with and in that group honed my skillset which allowed me to communicate with those of any ideology without ever feeling threatened or being threatening.

While the group is not as active as it used to be, it has created an army of people throughout the country that continues the civility path. We all try to follow the Coffee Party tenets.

We continue to promote articles, organizations, activities, and organizations that are bringing people together to create a better country. Giving the state of our politics there is a lot more continuous work that is necessary, and hence the reason I took this fork to be a part of the solution.

We would meet yearly in cities like Washington DC, Denver Colorado, Eugene Oregon, Portland, Chicago, Detroit, among others to constantly hone our tenets as the country's polarization evolved. It is clear the process must continue.

Coffee Party Tenets

The simplicity and humanity within the Coffee Party USA tenets make it easy to sell. And when used diligently it is failure proof.

A dedication to civility, learning, authenticity, and transparency breeds trust even for those who may disagree with you.

Mission Statement: Coffee Party USA empowers and connects communities to reclaim our government for the people.

Vision Statement: Coffee party envisions a nation of diverse communities sharing a culture of informed public engagement that sustains a tradition where our solemn right to vote is the currency of our democracy.

Civility Pledge: As a member or supporter of the Coffee Party, I pledge to conduct myself in a way that is civil, honest, and respectful toward people with whom I disagree. I value people from different cultures, I value people with different ideas, and I value and cherish the democratic process.

Core Values: We live the values we want to see in our government.

Civility: We empathize and engage with one another exercising humility, listening, honesty and respect, in order to provide an emotionally safe environment even when we disagree.

Continuous Learning: We seek the truth, learn the facts, and share with others to make informed decisions relevant to the ongoing improvement of ourselves, the nation and our shared, overlapping lives.

Authenticity & Transparency: Because we are human, in our genuine quest to restore our republic's representative democracy we may stumble, but we will do so in plain sight, with trust and expecting a hand up from one another.

Integrity & Clarity: We say what we mean, and do what we say and in so doing we strive to create a country that is whole and undiminished.

Inclusiveness: We reach out, engage and connect with people from diverse communities, backgrounds, cultures and political perspectives.

Transpartisan / independence: We engage in political and social bridge-building for the sake of finding solutions to common problems, working above and beyond ideological dogmas, putting the country first.

It is not easy to live up to these tenets. One must be intentional. It is the only way one can bridge the divide between ideologies real and implied.

What I have discovered in speaking to people of all stripes is that it is not a cliché to state that we are all seeking the same thing expressed differently.

Once one comes to that realization intentionality in the process is much less difficult. It becomes easier to concentrate less on self because self is not all that different from the other. Make that your epiphany.

Chapter 3: First understand who we are

I do not play chess but if I did, I am sure I would equate today's politics with some three-dimensional version of it. And in the game, the middle-class and poor are likely to be ill-prepared to win. Centrism has powerful allies.

This must be repeated ad-nauseam, the American political game is played between two rails both moving biased to the right. Parties attempt to keep the flanks on their specific side of the rail to prevent derailment. Over time this is consequential. Like the frog that stays in water as the temperature gradually increases to its eventual cooking, our political reality is sealing our economic demise.

We attempt to maintain the status quo by steering everyone to a mythical center, that rightward skewing center. Stray too far from it and we incur the wrath of the "liberal" punditry and media. One should not forget that Donny Deutch, a "liberal pundit" who at times has good Democratic marketing ideas, once blurted out that he would vote for Donald Trump if Bernie Sanders or Elizabeth Warren won the nomination.

But this should not be a surprise. Maurice Mitchell, National Director of the Working Families Party made a statement at Netroots Nation 2019 that caught my attention.

Encapsulated within is the analysis that should define the Progressive narrative and path.

America cannot survive if it does not shift to the Progressive side. The only way that could happen is by saying and standing up for what we want.

There are a lot of folks who are attempting to put fear into Progressives to stop us from doing what is needed under the pretense of unity, a false unity.

> *Whenever anybody talks about unity, it's actually a surrender. And whenever anyone talks about ideology, they are always talking about Progressives. For some reason, the radical centrists do not have an ideology.*

> *You are being way too ideological because we're talking about our values. They are talking about their values. They are talking about their corporate values. So, to me, the intervention needs to be like we need to demystify some of these terms and stop pretending that these are neutral terms. These are loaded terms. These are political terms that are designed to steer us towards a particular politic. And we need to resist that.*

When former President Obama said, "This is still a country that is less revolutionary than it is interested in improvement. ... The average American doesn't think we have to completely tear down the system and remake it," at the Democracy Alliance, he was not speaking for the people Mitchell was talking about nor the wants of most Americans polled. It was an ideology he was projecting on us all.

Billionaire Michael Bloomberg had no problem with a regressive soda tax but will spend millions to buy the Democratic Party Presidential nomination to oppose a wealth tax most Americans support as well as other progressive policy proposals. He entered the 2020 Democratic Primary to make life better for who? He entered the race to help steer the Democratic debate to keep it from becoming too progressive. He was likely more successful than most would like to admit.

Stated in many past articles is the fact that most Americans support progressive policies. Yet we have a crop of politicians going out of their way to tell Americans why they should not want these policies with misleading narratives.

- Free tuition will give rich kids an unfair break.
- Paying off student debt is a moral hazard.
- A Green New Deal is just too expensive.
- Medicare for All will raise your taxes.
- Giving everyone the option for childcare is not realistic.
- A living wage is too expensive for employers.

Here is an interesting fact. The last time the federal minimum wage was changed was on July 24th, 2009, more than 10 years ago. Just like Social Security is indexed to inflation for older people, shouldn't the minimum wage be as well?

Centrism dictates that we believe that the above policies are unattainable, unaffordable, or simply wrong. Neither under our current economic paradigm nor a more equitable one is that true.

We exist in a closed economic loop based on the economic model we choose. It is beyond the scope of this book to detail economic models but examples that follow give some flavor. It is all about how we choose to distribute. For each of the policies enumerated above, there is a cost associated with not providing them.

As an example. Not having free college tuition means that corporations and the rich pay less in taxes which end up in the hands of shareholders and the wealthy. Students who must take out loans must delay or downsize expenditures as they pay loans back. Interest from the loans in the aggregate goes to the rich. This dynamic creates three things. Corporations get trained employees on the cheap. Wealthy people get paid on all sides (fewer taxes, interest payments), and reduced economic activity stunts the growth of the many.

A similar dynamic occurs with Medicare for All which I discussed with the co-founder of the Center for Economic and Policy Research Economist Dr. Dean Baker on Politics Done Right.

Dr. Baker detailed why Senator Elizabeth Warren is correct in the way she addressed the question about tax increases with Medicare for All. Most importantly, allowing ourselves to acquiesce to the fallacy that we cannot afford it means we are complicit in the early deaths of many of our fellow Americans.

Again, the failure to provide every single progressive policy has an opportunity cost. And the beneficiaries are always corporations and the rich. Centrism is the engine that makes the will of the Right palatable. Unfortunately, the outcome is not indigestion but permanent disability.

Progressives know within their core that these values are attainable. The market for those ideas is not the Centrists that will continue to sabotage any attempt to fully attain them. We must market them to those on the Right who are living the conditions that would be solved by the policies. After all, the Centrists are already informed. Their interests are simply less altruistic than Progressives as they do not necessarily believe in a truly egalitarian society.

We must develop methods and techniques to win over many on the Right. There is a huge market there to create true Progressives.

Chapter 4: Understanding their frame

If one is on the left, understanding the driving force, the fuel that ignites the passions of the right is imperative. In simple terms, it is fear.

The Right is taught to fear just about every action on the Left. Those who manufacture the fear for their Right-Wing followers manipulate at all cost. This can become dangerous if not fatal.

Productive conversations with Right-Wing conservatives require understanding their fears and how to build trust before the fear blocks the conversations.

One must understand, every few weeks a new fear or a permutation of the fear is placed in circulation to keep them in a critical state. That is the reason every December the Liberal War on Christmas is recycled.

Examples of their fears are never ending as they are attached to resources invested in making sure they remain in that state. It is corrosive but does not have to be durable. We can change that.

The liberal caricature

Listen to Fox News, Right-Wing radio, or Right-Wing blogs. It is not hard to understand why those attached to those sources of information are terrified of liberals.

I am also terrified of those people they are describing. According to those sources of information liberals want to kill them.

Right-Wingers and Conservatives are made to believe that they care for America and are its sole protectors. It is the reason they believe they must exercise their 2nd Amendment rights which prevents a tyrannical government subservient to liberals from running over them. I always wondered if they really believed an AK-47 could go up against an armored tank or an F-16. And if not are they not living a false sense of security?

They have been led to believe that good public policy is an infringement of their freedoms. Ironically, they do not seem to understand that much of what they depend on is in fact public policy, from Social Security, to Medicare, to Medicaid.

They see a program like Medicare for All as taking away their freedom, their ability to choose. Ironically, oblivious to them because of how their media indoctrinate them is the reality.

Private insurance companies are the ones restricting their freedom. While they may have a choice of insurance companies, it is the insurance companies that decide which doctors they can see, which medicines they can take, and what procedures they can have. To them freedom is selecting who they want as their enslaving master.

Medicare for All alternatively gives them the freedom to choose their doctors, doctor selected medicines, and procedures. That the reality is diametrically opposite to their beliefs applies to just about everything they fear.

The violent-black-people fear

The violent-black-people fear has been used from the inception of the country. It has always been used as a means of controlling all people. If black people are dehumanized and thought of as violent and dangerous, it automatically creates a failsafe against crosspollination of ideas and "willful-genetics" between people.

What is true is that if one bases their fear on who is harmed by whom, reality says that black people should be the ones who are afraid.

It was always a myth that white women needed to fear being raped by black men. What is true is from the founding fathers to slavery to the Jim Crow days and beyond, white men raping black women have been prevalent. And the evidence lives on in the genetics of black people.

The above reality is best articulated by author/poet Caroline Randall Williams in her widely read New York Times article titled "You Want a Confederate Monument? My Body Is a Confederate Monument"

> *I have rape-colored skin. My light-brown-blackness is a living testament to the rules, the practices, the causes of the Old South.*

If there are those who want to remember the legacy of the Confederacy, if they want monuments, well, then, my body is a monument. My skin is a monument. ...

I am a black, Southern woman, and of my immediate white male ancestors, all of them were rapists. My very existence is a relic of slavery and Jim Crow.

According to the rule of hypodescent (the social and legal practice of assigning a genetically mixed-race person to the race with less social power) I am the daughter of two black people, the granddaughter of four black people, the great-granddaughter of eight black people. Go back one more generation and it gets less straightforward, and more sinister. As far as family history has always told, and as modern DNA testing has allowed me to confirm, I am the descendant of black women who were domestic servants and white men who raped their help.

It is an extraordinary truth of my life that I am biologically more than half white, and yet I have no white people in my genealogy in living memory. No. Voluntary. Whiteness. I am more than half white, and none of it was consensual.

White Southern men — my ancestors — took what they wanted from women they did not love, over whom they had extraordinary power, and then failed to claim their children.

How can you really fear a people who have allowed their domination for over 400 years both economically and socially and through slavery for a substantial portion of that time? How can you fear a people who have allowed a criminal justice system to incarcerate more of them per capita than any other racial or ethnic group? How can you fear a people when 85% of murders are white on white? How can you fear a people when most of the drugs that kill, legal or illegal are created, or not produced by those you are told to fear? How can you fear those who do not produce the weapons that kill on our streets?

The irrational fear is a method of control not of black people but of the majority population, white people. But too many leave the false narrative unanswered because it makes many uncomfortable.

Not dealing with that discomfort head on is harmful. It allows white people the false belief that their positions on race is justified and moral.

One can communicate truth in a respectful and nonjudgmental manner. One cannot completely fault anyone from their lived and indoctrinated experience.

We all must be deprogrammed from the many fallacies that have been instilled in our psyche for many reasons. Unfortunately, none of those reasons make the lives of the poor and middle-class any better. Instead, it ensures we take our eyes off the ball, the ones that oppress many. If we are fighting each other based on race and other attributes, we do not have the time to analyze the genesis of our real problems.

The browning-of-America fear

Since the creation of America, the majority population was led to believe that they were entitled to something most never had or got. But at least their hue gave them first dibs most of the times.

As America is becoming browner with interracial procreation, faster birth rates among people of color, and more people of color migrating to America, the entitlement became more diluted for many reasons.

As racial equilibrium is reached there is no dominant stakeholder. A city like Houston Texas is roughly a third each white, black, and Latino. As such, the interests of all are considered which ultimately lends itself to a more egalitarian society all else being equal. But make equality and equal access to success a negative for the white population and suddenly people of color are taking away white people's birthright. It is a false narrative because they were fighting for something they never really had. And that is the magic of dividing people on easily definable lines, race, religion, etc. It creates conflicts between groups that should be working together to demand from those controlling our economic system the spoils we all earned.

We could enumerate fear after fear that is used to control people in our system, but it is out of the scope of this book. Suffice it to say that the winning formula for a time was to aggregate white people on many fears. Make those fears less sinister by including acceptable token people of color who are willingly ignorant or advantaged financially. And then in that manner one can control the fearful and the feared.

The number of black and brown "actors" who are using social media to con white people into maintaining their belief that their false fears or racist beliefs are justified, have exploded. It is all part of the marketing.

Liberals & Progressives are anti-religion

I would wager that when it comes to ideology that the church is populated with both **Lefties** and **Righties** and every ideological permutation in between. But for one to hate one's human brother and sister, it is essential that a narrative is built about something fundamental to one's self that the other is attempting to remove, curtail, control, or destroy.

Making the Liberal/Progressive godless creates a boogie person deserving of attack, hate, and scorn. After all, they want to take away something that is intrinsic to your being. What is ironic is religious Liberals believe the tenets they stand for follow more the teachings of just about every religion.

Before becoming a Humanist, I was a Christian. In fact, back home I had even preached on a youth Sunday. I remember being shocked that after giving a short sermon I prepared just before church, a long line of people came up to the pulpit to give their lives to the Lord. I was young and when I saw that, I was genuinely scared.

The funny thing is I did not know what I feared until I came to the United States. It is then that I learned something about the susceptibility of the mind to cues of any kind.

My experience has taught me that there are two mindsets. Each one must be approached differently.

The first mindset is comfortable to accept everything on faith. They believe in a domination hierarchy that represent their trusted sources, their pastor, a think tank, etc. They are generally immutable unless the trusted hierarchy is broken. Getting to them requires discrediting the hierarchy, a difficult task.

The second mindset is fact-based. Interestingly, you find that mindset in every ideology but at different levels. Consensus is easier to reach here as civil and respectful dialogue usually suffice.

Liberals & Progressives are baby killers

The abortion debate has been the coup de grace of the Right. It was the one absolute difference that they could grab on to.

They have made the fetus a human and as such abortion is murder. And lest Liberals do not know, there is a commandment against that.

Of course, that argument fails as they have attached themselves to a corresponding business first tenant which defeats their life at all cost tenet.

Business first policies which in America means low taxes and lacking social services likely cause more loss of born life than abortions ever could.

Texas is a very red state that purports itself to cherish life. Yet it is the state with the largest number of uninsured Americans. What is evil is that the Federal Government offered what is known as the Medicaid Expansion to the Affordable Care Act that would have likely made it possible to insure every Texan. It was free for the first three years. Thereafter it cost the state 10% of the medical outlays. The Texas Republican Legislature rejected it.

That act caused the deaths of thousands of Texans every year simply from the lack of insurance. What cannot be counted is the number who died from the additional stress and suffering because they lived in a state that did not care about their well-being.

Is not voluntary manslaughter defined as causing the death of someone knowingly. Maybe it is time that we start to hold elected officials to some modification of that law.

Many on the Right are yearning for a dialogue

I talk directly and indirectly to hundreds of people every week. Right-wingers troll me ad nauseam. Recently, something strange has begun; I find conservatives trolling my trolls in my defense as I continue to expound our progressive mantra. Many are open for a dialogue.

It is clear to me from my experience in my own community, people who stumble onto my radio show Politics Done Right, and from a recently attended Bridge Alliance Conference that the fever is breaking. People yearning for dialogue need a path to spaces where they can "blossom."

I think one of the biggest mistakes we make, irrespective of ideologies, is allowing the plutocracy to use the differences between people to maintain and increase their power, the good old divide and conquer.

If we are fighting one another we give those who are inflicting the damage on us all a pass. We take our eyes off the ball.

Progressives and conservatives have a genuine fear of each other. I think it is irrational, but it is by design. If you watch Fox News you would fear Progressives as well.

Recently a caller to Politics Done Right made several points. She first made it clear she was on the right. But then she explained that she came to the realization that it was less about the parties and more about class. More importantly, she realized that "others" are instigating. If we are fighting one another we cannot fight those responsible for our ills.

This woman's call mimicked many emails I get from conservative listeners as well. They are not crazy. They want a conversation where they think they are not looked down on.

It is not important whether that is true or not. They have a network they still trust that reinforces many fallacies that become their reality.

So how do you talk to the Right side?

Remember these words; patience, humility, listen, thick skin, selflessness, and genuine compassion. Those are tenets that are generally not American. I must admit it was not very me either.

The American birthright is that it is on top of the pyramid. Humility is unnecessary because everyone tries to please her.

Americans do not have to listen to opposition because they have the power financially and militarily. They are used to everyone bending to them.

Americans never needed to develop callouses, a thick skin. Why? They are untouchable in the grand scheme of the world.

Patience is unnecessary because if Americans are made to wait, they just find a rationale to take it. Colombia told us we could not build a canal through a piece of their territory ideal for a canal. That territory in Colombia became the country, Panama, that signed a treaty, henceforth, the Panama Canal.

Compassion is not a necessary deed because America's word cannot be disputed. If she says she is compassionate she is.

And selflessness? Be for real, it is all about America!

That is the American tenet. What is amazing is with all the disparities, racial tensions, and other problems in America, the American as seen in Latin America, the Caribbean, and many other countries were that monolithic composite of those characteristics.

The defined characteristics of what it means to be an American works only on the outside. It is the America that many of us envisioned. It was powerful and those who make it here become American.

But there is a problem. When every American feels they are exceptional yet have many differences in values and morality, that exceptionalism becomes a weakness that can be exploited or worse. It can be fatal.

Since no one needs to have patience, practice humility, listen to the other, develop a thick skin to hear things that make one uncomfortable, display genuine compassion, or think about only self, few do them. After all, while the Right is strong as they articulate individualism and individual freedom, many on the old Left while not preaching it, live it.

Those on the Left then need to accept an inconvenient truth. On the human level and on the things, everyone wants, they are not all that far apart even as their differences are exploited and magnified for a specific purpose.

Right Wing journalist would go to a Progressive campus and ask many questions that show that Progressives are oblivious to reality. I recall one in which they asked a Progressive student if he would sign a petition against a dangerous sounding chemical, H-2-O. The guy was happy to sign because he did not realize H-2-O was the chemical formula for water. The same kind of pranks have been done in Conservative areas to make it seem that Conservatives are dumb and uninformed. The reality is that on both sides we have too many poorly read people that are simply being led to their positions devoid of individual analytical thought.

On the Left it is easy to disregard that similarity because we know that the tenets of the Left are generally more fact and data based. Again, the Right feels the same way. After all, their "fact-based" organizations like the Heritage Foundation gives them plausibility with believable data.

To be clear, there is no doubt that in these time, truth, reality, and data is on the side of the Left, the Progressive side. Unfortunately, that reality is a danger to too many of the people who control our economic system.

To further understand the chasm between Right and Left in the last fifty plus years one must understand a few things. As Americans started asking more and more questions about what is fair and also the "why" of many of the country's economic tenets, the corporate powers started to worry. People would start demanding their worth.

And who would come to the rescue? Lewis Powell, a Democrat. Why do I point out his party? Because later it will be clear that a major argument to use with those on the right is the acknowledgment that as Left and Right fight, the folks at the top or race-less, party-less, ideology-less, and care solely about the green paper.

The Powell Memo illustrates the fear that Lewis Powell, a corporate lawyer, and member of the boards of various corporations had for the masses. Powell was subsequently confirmed as a Supreme Court justice appointed by Richard Nixon.

Powell lays out the game plan. The Powell Memo is a plan that was forward-looking. It is a plan that so far has been well implemented. How did they do it? Here are two paragraphs from the awfully long document.

> *While neither responsible business interests, nor the United States Chamber of Commerce, would engage in the irresponsible tactics of some pressure groups, it is essential that spokesmen for the enterprise system — at all levels and at every opportunity — be far more aggressive than in the past.*

> *There should be no hesitation to attack the Naders, the Marcuses and others who openly seek destruction of the system. There should not be the slightest hesitation to press vigorously in all political arenas for support of the enterprise system. Nor should there be reluctance to penalize politically those who oppose it.*

The success of the Powell Memo is in the ubiquity of its implementation.

They created think tanks responsible for dispersing misleading information with a false cloak of authenticity. The Heritage Foundation is a classic example of this. They took control of the airwaves to disperse misleading information (e.g., talk radio, Fox News, CNBC, etc.). A relenting Chamber of Commerce uses corporate monies to bully policy and politicians that squeeze the masses (e.g., support for free trade agreements, outsourcing etc.).

They infiltrated college campuses with directed research for planned outcomes. They infiltrated the elementary and secondary schools' textbook evaluation process to attempt Right Wing indoctrination. They used graduate business schools to indoctrinate students on an irresponsible form of capitalism. They flooded the country with books and paid advertising promoting their message. They continue to destroy unions.

The implementation has been successful thus far. The problem is that in Powell's days there was no Internet. There was no way to form disjointed communities in mass that could rise-up when knowledge was not controlled in a top-down manner. A new tactic had to be added. This new tactic is not new. It is the war to divide and conquer.

In Chapter 4: Understanding their frame we pointed out the frame under which many on the Right view Progressives. This is a direct result of the intricacies of the messaging and institutional elements placed into action by the Powell Memo.

Here is an elemental thought process.

Absolute Truths:

1. Climate change is real and quantifiable.
2. The burning of fossil fuels causes climate change.
3. A feature of our economic system is vast wealth inequality.
4. Our economic system is incentivized to have employees work at a discount with the spoils going to shareholders and executives.
5. White supremacy is real and an economic tool that ultimately favors a few and hurts the average white person as well.
6. The country needs immigration to maintain its current living standard.
7. Universal healthcare is more efficient and less expensive.
8. Charter school in the aggregate are not better than public schools and serve to enrich a connected few, the shareholders and overpaid executives of the schools.
9. Capitalism has nothing to do with democracy and free enterprise.

Grey Areas:

1. Is abortion wrong?
2. Is prayer in school wrong?

3. Is gun control unconstitutional?
4. How is freedom defined?
5. What role should government play in our lives?

The list is just partial but sufficient. I have divided the topics over which the Right and the Left argue as **Absolute Truths** and **Grey Areas**.

Everything in the **Absolute Truth** list are mathematically quantifiable or logically deducible with real world actualizations. The **Grey Area** list depends on things like faith, interpretations of ambiguities, an outright chosen view based on one's personal value set.

The modus operandi since the inception of the Powell Memo was to associate a Conservatism with a set of values and intertwine it with the economic priorities of a few. It was no longer policy a-la-carte that could stand up on its own merit.

That was the perfect juxtapositions for those who make faith their commanding north star, everything else in the menu must go together.

That is completely different from the Progressive mindset. Math and absolute logic are the prevailing tenets.

This is not to deny that the same prejudices and other societal-instilled tenets do not form the core of the Progressive person. The difference is that Progressives do not attempt to find a way to justify or codify their prejudices. They ignore them while Conservatives try to justify them. And that is the intersectionality from whence communication can occur in a very human and honest manner.

In Chapter 2 I discussed my path from being a homophobe to redemption and atonement. I had a deep flaw that needed to be corrected and I had to humble myself, be thick-skinned to accept the blow-back, be compassionate with those who had not yet seen the light, be selfless understanding it was not about me but who I previously hurt.

That story shows that I survived doing a 180 on a belief system that was simply wrong. Not only that, but most of my friends held the same belief that I did. I was the only one immediately changing. I did not only survive the peer pressure but many figured if a pigheaded Black/Caribbean/Latino could see the light maybe there was something there. So, to many I became the catalyst to speed up their enlightenment.

When I speak to Conservatives, I do the following.

1. I listen attentively. I am not just hearing. I am trying to understand the genesis of their thought. Is it just spin? Is it a true belief? Are they telling me what they think I want to hear? Are they trying to just touch my buttons?

2. I generally affirm nothing that I know as fact. I start asking them to elaborate on the statements and tenets they make. All the while I am outwardly respectful even if their initial comments were verifiably from another dimension.

3. As a fallible human like everyone else, I can always find a personal failure to equate to some failure I would want them to consider in their premise.

4. Generally, by then a genuine mutual respect starts to develop and guards start coming down. To be clear, I never go into these conversations with my guard up. In fact, I am sometimes happy when they can correct me on any valid point because they do not feel one is attempting to play some intellectually superior card (which I never play).

5. Somewhere during the conversation, when possible, I make it clear that I am not

trying to get them to change their party affiliation or self-defined ideology. My goal is always a policy per policy argument. The dirty little secret is the reason a Powell Memo was necessary is when one checks out the needs and wants of most Americans, it always turns out that sans abortion, gun control, and church stuff, most people ultimately support Progressive policies.

There are several things one must be ready for when having these conversations. Always remember this is never about self but about moving the notch in having civil discourse and moving policies that move us all forward.

Change almost never occur in one sitting or one conversation. You are mostly planting seeds that reality will fertilize. I have had people look me up weeks, months, or years later with an epiphany.

Some people are immutable and are simply sycophants to an ideology illogically at all cost.

The indoctrination of the population by the Powell Memo did not occur overnight. While some of us see the light and snap out of the fog, it does not work in that manner for most.

Patience and humility is important. Expect even those you think have shown some level of flexibility to revert to form several times before becoming independent and impervious to peer pressure.

Do not ever get discouraged. The process of change especially in these times is difficult. I once believed that when everyone had access to limitless data one could use for research that misinformation would go out the door. Never would I have imagined that there are those putting the same energy or more into misinformation.

There are virtually unlimited resources for those who profit from misinformation. And that is why Progressives can leave no stone unturned. We must engage everyone understanding that we must work hard to prove that ultimately humanity can trump money.

Chapter 5: Stories

Stories are powerful. I love to communicate to my radio and internet audience with stories. Most of us live our lives in stories.

I have had hundreds of encounters with Right-Wingers of all stripes. Some were violent. Some went out of their way to make me comfortable even if I was the sole "pinko liberal."

People find it hard to believe. By being opened to the dialogue, I have found commonality few immediately understand. But by the end it will not be hard to infer why.

Explaining Medicare for All

I was sitting in one of my favorite Coffee Shops. Before the pandemic I just about lived in there till one o'clock. I would then go to my home studio to do the Politics Done Right show.

I would return to the Coffee Shop many times again in the late afternoons. On this specific day a woman came and sat next to me.

"I see you here all of the time," she said sort of soliciting an informative reply.

I told her I was a national blogger and radio/media show host and loved the environment. I get a lot of blog ideas from a myriad of people I meet there. Many have become subjects in my blogs or shows, anonymous most of the times of course.

We started talking about healthcare. I do not remember how we got there. But we both agreed that the health insurance system was a mess.

The woman thought she hated Obamacare even though she was on a particularly good employer-based insurance plan. I have spoken to many people about health care. It is one of my most important topics of conversations.

I asked many questions. What about her insurance did she not like? I got the standard response. The premium was too high. The deductibles were too high. The co-pays were a nuisance. She hated having to go through the ringer to see a specialist. And she hated having to select alternative drugs because the insurance company only allowed a specific one. The woman hated that she had to constantly check to see if a specific doctor was on her plan.

I told my new friend that my wife had Lupus and because she has a preexisting condition that it has been hard to get insurance and as a self-employed business owner the yearly increases were terrible.

I did not yet tell the woman that we were on Obamacare and the value compared to how things were before was orders of magnitude better. I did not want to do anything to change the flow of the discourse.

I pointed out her plan was no different than Obamacare.

"Really?" she asked sort of in shock.

At this point because I was so attentive as I listened without offering any opinions the woman likely took my response not as one favoring Obamacare but just stating a fact. I am sure she thought I was one of the few black Republicans in the community.

I asked her what she would like in a plan. She wanted no deductible, small copay, the ability to select the doctor of her choice and the drug of her doctor's choice. In effect she wanted to escape the chains of the insurance company.

I told her she was describing the concept for Medicare for All. She gave me a confused look. I also pointed out that like Obamacare insurance companies could not rescind the policy or place caps on how much they were willing to pay for her care. At this point it was clear that she was having a mental conversation.

I felt guilty because I am sure that with all the talking I was doing mostly by having her answer her own questions and having her tweak her answers with further questions for answers requiring clarification, she was sure that I was just an analytical Republican.

The most important question had to do with the option to choose. She said she did not want socialized health insurance because she wanted the freedom to choose health insurance companies that best fulfill her needs.

I asked her what happens if her needs change in the middle of the year. She had a blank look.

It was time for me to come clean because it was time to go a bit deeper.

"Mam, I think I need to tell you something," I said. "I am Progressive Liberal, a real lefty."

The woman turned cherry red in her face. She could not speak for a few seconds. The piercing stare eye to eye seemed like an eternity.

The woman then blurted out, "But you are so nice!"

I could not help but laugh out loud. I told her the caricature she sees portrayed in Right Wing Media is just that, a caricature. I told her she should go have lunch with our local Liberal Ladies Who Lunch.

I wanted to continue the conversation and she did too. I asked her to please tell me which system gives her the most freedom. Is the one that you have to shop around for on a yearly basis which comes the closest to her needs freer than the one where you go to the doctor of your choice who can prescribe the medicine or procedure they deem more fit? Of course, she picked the latter which is Medicare for All.

By then she had already convinced herself that Medicare for All was the best choice. But while intellectually she could have made the leap, ideology had her stating what was a fact to her. That will cost too much, and all our insurance would go up.

I asked her by how much she thought her premium would go up. She said 10 to 20%. I asked her if she would give someone $200 to pay a $160 bill. She said that made no sense.

"Isn't that what insurance companies do?" I asked.

She agreed.

"But don't they have to put away for the rainy day?" she asked.

That was her way to talk about managing risk.

"If there was only one entity paying the bill wouldn't all the cost get spread across millions of people?" I asked.

After the conversation, it was clear the seed was planted, fertilized, and sprouting. She had proving to herself that Single Payer Medicare for All was the best answer.

I am sure her husband will have her second guessing herself. But I am confident that the tenor of our discourse made her feel empowered as she should.

My new friend may not become a healthcare activist with her husband (to keep the peace) but I am sure she will never look at health insurance the same again. It was clear she saw the utter lack of logic of private insurance as the method of paying for one's healthcare.

Talking to descendants of Daniel Boone

A few years ago, during the heat of the healthcare debate, I attended a Tea Party event in Houston, TX at Just-A-Bar pub. At the time I was doing a lot of blogging on Obamacare.

So, why would this black man go to a Tea Party event at a pub on the outskirts of Houston? Well, I was also invited to go meet a militia in Waco Texas. My wife forbade me from attending that meeting. It was during the heat of the Tea Party movement when some of the most vile and racist attacks on President Obama was in full vogue.

So, I guess the Tea Party meeting in a bar may have been a bit safer. Then again, I did see the Confederate flag on the wall. I must admit, I never let symbols, and epithets defer me from a mission.

I was frustrated that those who would benefit the most from Obamacare were some of the biggest objectors. At the time I was also a part of a group of prolific CNN iReporters. One of them asked me if I would speak to these Tea Party folk from my perspective. I figure it was time to use my Coffee Party USA skills.

I am used to going into environments where I am the raisin in a sea of milk. Moreover, this raisin was as Progressive as one can get. Yes, one of those Pinko Liberals.

I went in with my camera and was ready for an interview. I wrote the following then,

> *All attendees were friendly, engaged, and welcoming. One issue that stood out was the disdain they had for the government. In the various interviews I did as well as the taping of the event, I tried to ascertain if this disdain in their view was post-election of Obama or otherwise.*

> *The men interviewed are descendants of the famous Daniel Boone we all watched on TV. That the distrust of the government would lead well-meaning citizens to campaign against a healthcare policy that given their own current lack of healthcare coverage would be extremely beneficial to their health and economic wellbeing is incredulous. This is the level of what could only be considered an irrational distrust for a government when one cannot overtly see any negative effect this administration is having on these citizens either materially or socially.*

> *Though to many on the left this may seem like irrational paranoia, it is something*

> *that should be addressed lest these*
> *people's psyche continue to make*
> *themselves feel caged and marginalized.*
> *This is a common human behavior when*
> *any group feel themselves under attack*
> *however real or imagined.*

I expected to be upset at these people even though I had no intention of showing it. I thought I would be there for one hour. Instead I was there for north of five hours talking, debating, understanding, and learning how to best get through to their value set.

The one thing that stuck out to me is that they wanted me to know that they were not racist. The truth is just as I was a homophobe at a point in my life they were still racists who tried to mitigate it with treating me impeccably well not realizing that many of their statements made their true feelings as clear as I was black.

For me that was not important. I was on a mission to engage for a cause. My one hour with them turned into five hours because our curiosities of each other became genuine as commonalities were found.

At the end some acknowledged prejudices and expressed a need to change. The reality is they were unlikely to change immediately because of the comfort factor and peer pressure. But the fact that they legitimately realized that they needed to change, and that the system worked much differently than they thought was a start. I gave the dad a copy of my book and asked him to read it.

Acknowledgement is the most important step towards change so that is progress. I knew our communication made a difference.

In the process of talking, one of the men told me he was an engineer. I told him I was one as well and that I develop software as well.

A few weeks later I got a call from him that shocked me. He had a project he was working on and wanted to know if I was interested in being a part of it. That was huge. I was too busy to consider working with him. But by not standing my ground at the same time using the tenets I previously discussed, those doors opened.

Explaining immigration

I was on the phone doing Coffee Party USA business, when a man approached me. I think he wanted to talk politics but did not know where on the spectrum I fit. It was easy to discern that he was a Trump voter. MAGA and all.

I initially thought this Trump supporter was stuck in his ways. I could not believe that with all that had happened he could still embrace his guy.

Earlier on I remember he was defending the President on the premise that somehow his utterances would materialize. But it is on immigration where I think he had an epiphany. He was all in with the wall and bought into the fallacy that illegal immigration is a significant problem in the U.S.

How did he come to his epiphany? Respectful dialog planted seeds that were fertilized by an inherent curiosity. That led him to read other sources he could somewhat respect if he could confirm it was not some ultra-progressive source.

The Trump supporter found an article he could believe that pointed out the stark reality that America is not creating enough babies to take care of the older generation. He got it. But how would he get that new observation to square with his previous state of reality. It did not matter. The message reached him, and he was going to do something about it.

My friend showed up at Starbucks with a big grin.

"I want to talk to you about immigration," he said. "And you are going to like what I am going to say."

"Really?" I replied.

"We need immigration," he said. "Lots of it."

Suffice it to say; I was shocked. The Trump voter explained that we were on an unsustainable path. He realized that Social Security would go bankrupt if a lot of immigrants were not let into the country. He said he would write a piece for my blog detailing his thoughts on the issue.

A few days ago, sitting across from me on a shared table, he flipped his computer around.

"Here it is," he said. "Tell me what you think."

I read it. Absent a few 'erroneous facts' it is a negotiable concept. A Trump voter turned supporter of immigration will not have suggestions that a Democratic Socialist would. This was not empathy. This was transactional.

But if you can get Trump supporters to arrive at the tenet that immigration is good and immigrants are inherently good, that is a massive achievement.

My friend titled the piece "COME to AMERICA: Monetize Immigration" which I found amusing. Look, he is a Republican. His first paragraph starts with a false premise but ironically it had little impact on what he wants to accomplish with immigration.

> *America, we have a problem. Immigration is the foundation of America, but illegal immigration is growing exponentially, causing a political divide rooted in polarization without a pragmatic solution. The problem is not going away. America is now competing globally for our political and economic future. Let's change our paradigm. Let's grow America with human power.*

He starts in a place Progressives would mostly like or can live with to some extent.

> *At the moment, the illegal and legal immigration challenge is mired in endless debate and it is out of control because we are too focused on these tactical topics:*
>
> ***Strengthen the Border****- build the wall (physically and/or digitally)*
>
> ***Illegal Self-Deportation****- destroy incentives (anchor babies, access to benefits)*
>
> ***Improve Legal Immigration****- improve the legal process (use work visa)*

Use America's Military at Borders- *legal or civilian voluntary solution*

Mandate E-Verify- *end employer hiring of illegals with penalties*

Legalize with Amnesty- *settle the immediate population (maybe 20-40 million)*

Strengthen Interior Enforcement- *the most controversial (criminal targeting)*

Let's end the immigration debate. We no longer need to argue about open borders or the terminology of legal versus illegal immigration. Let's take control of the problem and address the big picture of how America can compete globally and thrive.

The Trump voter realized that immigration is also about growth and he modifies MAGA to Make America Grow Again. Is that not a much better connotation than the dog whistle? He writes that America is about solving Global problems and business. His 180-degree turn wants to brand America "Come to America."

> *America was founded on solving global problems, with its early message... "The Business of America is Business". How America has historically solved problems, innovated or created new technologies has always involved "thinking big" or attracting "big thinkers". Globally, in the big scheme of things, America needs more revenue sources and to capture revenue legally that builds our American brand- "Come to America."*

He writes that we should be there selling the America brand by letting folks know we want them. This man, this Trump voter, may not admit that he made a 180-degree turn. In fact, in his piece, one can detect that he is fighting with himself rhetorically as many times the false Right-Wing Trumpian narrative bleeds in gratuitously. He ends his piece with a paragraph I wish he would start narrating to the Trump and Right-Wing base.

> *I'm a conservative, libertarian who wants America to excel socially, politically and economically. I want America's global brand to prosper in the potential of human being- leveraging human nature and be globally competitive. I do not want immigration fears to dictate how we solve or delay solving America's immigration problem. We need to*

think big and we need to sell America's greatest value- our LIBERTY and RULE of LAW brand.

Most Liberals, Progressives, Democratic Socialists, and the general Left will scoff at his piece. I told him that as a white guy with Trumpian proclivities, he could be a bridge to many on his side with Progressives to come up with a solution all can accept. I told him I would share his piece with my Trumpian friends making its origin clear. They would likely listen to him as one of them. Every Right-Wing Republican whose read his piece, loved it.

Supporter of dumping asylum seekers on Sanctuary cities

I go to the gym several times a week. I usually stay in my zone blasting KPFT 90.1 FM's morning shows, The Attitude with Arnie Arnesen, The Thom Hartmann Program, and Democracy Now with Amy Goodman. Usually, I do not hear any of the surrounding conversations.

Thom Hartmann was talking to several callers who complained about the effectiveness of the Right-Wing media converting their friends and families into paranoid Right Wingers they did not recognize. My Bluetooth earbuds died as Democracy Now! was starting. As I did some butterflies, I overheard a Right-Wing Republican man speaking to a receptive man.

"I love what Trump is doing," the Republican said. "Send them all to those cities. They are sanctuaries anyway. Let them deal with them."

My blood started to boil. The Republican kept on escalating the rhetoric as he demeaned these immigrants, these asylum seekers. I could take it no more.

I walked up to the man and looked him sternly in the eyes. It seemed to shock him initially.

"Do you know how inhumane you sound?" I asked.

After stuttering for a while, he gave me the standard cop-out answer.

"I don't have any problem with these people," he said. "But we must first change the law. We must have laws, not open borders."

I told him that humaneness superseded laws. When people are in dire straits, we must act humanely first and adjust rules later.

He touched on crime, and I reminded him of several important logical conclusions that Fox News taught their viewers to ignore.

- Most undocumented immigrants want to do nothing to attract any attention that could get them deported. As such, they commit less crime and do not vote.
- While the European settlers came here, killed those who helped them survive initially, conquered the land (read stole the property), and enslaved an entire race to create a fast-growing economy, the asylum seekers only want a life of peace and a job. Shouldn't the need for atonement demand more from us?
- People like him who profess higher morals should consult the Bible and the words of Jesus Christ and ask if his behavior would mimic their own.

During the entire conversation I was firm but not rude nor did I raise my voice. My approach elicited a similar behavior from the Republican. It was clear that no one has ever confronted him in the manner that I did. I created an environment where he deservedly was on the defensive. But most importantly I did not allow an escalation into a shouting match. While he spoke, I listened intently, and in this case, I did not have to ask him to reciprocate the behavior. In other confrontations, I have had to ask for the same respect in listening that I afforded.

Look, I am sure I did not change this Republican's basal way of being. But I do know I planted seeds that any thinking human being however ideologically compromised would have cemented in their brains whether they acknowledged it or not.

After going back and forth for about twenty minutes we shook hands, he thanked me. I wondered if he realized he did that. Anyway, I did not react. I gave him a back slap, we smiled and then I took off.

These are perilous times. The Right is always ready to confront and bully. We must do the same for the soul of this country. Most people are good but ideologically empty and rudderless. Whoever is more effective in filling that vacuum wins. Progressives, we are the ones with the verifiable truth. We must fill the voids. But more importantly, for voids filled with poison, we must blow it out of there.

Constitutionality of healthcare as a right

My very Progressive program Politics Done Right has a substantial number of Conservative listeners. One of them called in about healthcare and likely did not get the response he expected.

A Conservative, Brad, called into Politics Done Right to challenge the constitutionality of healthcare as a right. He got more than he bargained for quickly.

"I hear you and others at that station say health care is a right," Brad said. "Am I correct about that?"

I confirmed that he was correct about what we stood for at our Progressive station KPFT 90.1 FM Houston.

"Maybe I just skimmed too quickly," Brad said. "But when I read the constitution, I didn't see the word healthcare. So how is it a right?"

I pointed out that the Constitution alluded to it when it speaks about the "general welfare." I told him that people who always use the Constitution literally are usually trying to restrict one's rights. Others take an expansive view of the constitution to give as many human rights as possible.

I made it noticeably clear that I cherished humanity more so than the piece of paper written over a couple hundred years ago. I explained some unfortunate truths about the constitution.

1. Women did not get the right to vote until 1920 with the 19th amendment.
2. Black people were considered three-fifths of a person.
3. Under current interpretation, an artificial entity. a corporation is given many of the same rights given to an American human being.

I told the caller that I err on the side of humanity, not the literal words of the Constitution.

Later the caller wanted to assure me that he was not the TEA Party type. I made it clear that I did not care because my goal is not to preach to the choir but to those who need to be convinced or converted.

Many Conservatives tend to listen to my show or watch it on Facebook Live, YouTube, Twitch, or Periscope. It was clear that a seed was planted; That is how we change minds, one at a time by engaging respectfully.

White supremacist caller

A Right-Wing white supremacist called into my Politics Done Right show recently. I pride myself on giving every caller the opportunity to present their point of view. But I am never shy about civilly and respectfully refuting them. And I did just that.

The white supremacist had a calm voice likely expecting a shouting match that would unravel me as he came across as the sane one. He got a dignified, schooling instead

The caller had an interesting definition of voter fraud. In his opinion, undocumented immigrants perpetrate voter fraud by birthing American citizens. And because supposedly immigrants mostly vote for Democratic candidates it is a problem.

Throughout the discourse, it was clear that the caller was concerned about the demographic makeup of America. He finally fessed up to it when I made a case for the undocumented immigrants' rights to stay in this country.

"Immigration should be culturally compatible," the white supremacist said. "So yes, it should be mostly European immigration as it was pre-1965."

When I told him, he believes America must be a white country and that he believes in white supremacy, I got the expected answer.

"But Egberto," the caller said. "That is how the country was founded."

Of course, he is right. But a country founded on an immoral foundation could not stand if immutable. America became a great nation because its flawed creation had clauses that allowed it to grow and change.

The person who called after the white supremacist scolded me for being too kind to someone he perceived as evil. **I explained that when I speak to callers like the one who called, I am not responding solely to him, but to the thousands who are listening, some still with formative minds.**

I am not trying to convert on the spot as that is never long-lasting. I am trying to plant seeds with the expectation that some will grow and bear fruit.

Republican caller admits to more in common with Progressives

A Republican caller called into Politics Done Right because he took exception to my statement that political parties are not responsive to their constituents. He said the Republican Party represents him well. By the end of the discussion, he agreed with this Progressive that we, citizens, have more in common than our commonality with any party.

The Republican caller was a first-time listener. He was happy to call in.

The caller started the conversation saying that unlike folks from other parties, he is happy with his. Why. He supports a big strong military, low regulations, and many other things we regularly discuss on PDR.

I started taking each one of the issues he agreed with and deconstructed them. In the case of a big strong military, I pointed out that there was nothing conservative about it. After all, they allow contractors to rob the hard-earned taxpayer money.

When he switched to regulations it was clear that when presented from an empathetic perspective, he could not help but agree that we needed regulations.

Soon after, the Republican caller decided after-all we had more in common. I have found that respectfully talking works often. You start changing minds and coexisting when all involved feel mutual respect.

My response to email from irate listener on my tax cut stance

A listener to my Politics Done Right show was so irate that she fired off an email to me to complain. "I happened to hear the end of your show today on my way home from work," she said, "And would have loved to call in to counter every one of your callers." She thinks we are wrong about Trump's tax cut fraud.

Unfortunately, she did not call in because I would have loved to engage her. She believes the makers/takers myth. Worse, she thinks that those who are making the most unequivocally deserve it. I love when people like Linda make contact. We can only make a change if we go beyond the feel-goodness of being validated by our choir.

I will not judge Linda for the email she fired off even as it knocks a large percentage of Americans on false premises. It is evident she is educated by misinforming agents. One should judge her, however, based on her response after one presents her with the truth.

Linda's email

> I happened to hear the end of your show today on my way home from work and would have loved to call in to counter every one of your callers.
>
> One caller was upset because of changes in the estate tax. A tax that should be

eliminated for all income brackets. The caller, and you, only mentioned that the "rich" would not have to pay estate tax until it was over $5.4 million. What you failed to bring up, is that also means that the middle class family that leaves any amount under $5.4 million, do not have to pay tax. The "rich" will be the only one paying estate tax. You said all this "lost income" could go to pay off college debt or public assistance programs. Why should anyone have to pay tax on an estate that is taxed to death before you die? And you think our hard-earned money should go to pay off college debt. Well, tough. No one paid for my or my children's education. Why should I have to pay off a debt that someone else got themselves into? If they don't want student debt, they should go to a trade school. I go out and bust my butt at work. Why should I want to go along with Bernie's "Income Redistribution" plan? You said the new tax plan would be giving money to the rich. Actually, it would be allowing the income earners to keep what they earn, instead of allowing the leaches of the country to steal it.

Your show callers and you all talk about income inequality. Well, duh, nothing is equal in this world. So you think the rocket scientist and the burger flipper should have the same income? When did it become a bad thing for a company to actually make money? The workers that don't like the salary are free to go elsewhere. There will be lots of other people that want the job. And, if you want equality, how about if we all pay a flat percentage tax. Every single wage earner should pay the same. No more freebies or tax breaks for the half of the country that doesn't pay any tax. How about all the lazy people that sit at home on welfare get off their butt and get a job. Or, sit down and get a job. I am 66 years old and have worked since I was 16. I'll be damned before I give up what I work for without a fight. Your listeners, and Bernie supporters, all have been led to believe that everyone owes you something. The only thing you are owed, is what you earn for yourself.

So, needless to say, I didn't hear anything on your program that would lead me to listen.

My Response

Linda,

Before I respond to the meat of your email, I want to tell you a little bit about me. You see, just my being tends to have some people create preconceived notions of what informs my position. So, I want to dispel that up front. I've never received handouts from the government. For several years I have been in the highest *marginal tax bracket but with my voluntary change in profession that is no longer the case.*

Before I became a full-time blogger/radio host/political activist, I was an entrepreneur who owned a software development company. I have created dozens of products used all over the world, in oil companies, airplane manufacturers, NASA, POS, and more. I designed, developed, wrote, and supported all these products myself. They were my brainchild that paid for my home and put my daughter through school for her undergraduate degree. And since no bank would lend me money, I built the company on 18% to 22% credit card debt even though I've always had perfect credit.

Giving the narrative and tone of your email I needed you to know that my empathy, compassion, morals, and care for those with lesser means were neither self-serving nor based on economic ignorance.

First of all, the estate tax as it is, only affects those who would inherit more than $5.4 million. In 2013 alone 20 small businesses and family-owned farms paid the estate tax. Just 5,500 of the nation's 2.7 million estates will owe estate taxes. The estate tax is a mathematical necessity for any capitalist country to survive. If a small segment of a society grows faster financially than the rest, the mathematical reality is eventually that model caves because the masses are left continuously with less. The reality of that math has become evident already.

I did say the lost income could defer college costs and other safety net programs. Just like others invested in our generation, we must invest in those behind us.

Many Baby Boomers took advantage of the G.I. Bill, Pell Grants, low college tuition, and societal investments in programs to give a hand up. When it was our turn, we bought into Reagan's low taxes and supply-side fraud that is responsible for the wealth & income disparity today.

Many call the states the laboratories. There is an experiment that many are not talking about. It's Kansas vs. California. Suffice it to say, Kansas proved that the theory of the Right is a failure when put into full effect. The converse was true for California; Progressive policies are proven and work as they depend on math and science, not on some uncorroborated jive.

We have asked subsequent generations to pay more for everything so we could get lower taxes. We then ask why many cannot get up and launch themselves.

You speak about working hard for your money and not wanting to pay off someone else's debt. You went through your formative years, given your age you revealed, when taxes were at the proper levels. As such, you benefitted from a society that saw you as an investment. Politicians funded elementary, middle, and high school and college. We should want to pay it forward.

I respect your work. But you should recognize the work and contribution of others as well. You should realize that many do not get paid commensurate with their value or work output. I created dozens of products and made good money doing it.

Many, like stockbrokers and bankers, produce services that in no way provide similar value. Yet, they make orders of magnitude more. That is the defect in our economic system that intelligent taxation must mitigate.

Just like I do not believe a burger flipper and a rocket scientist are entitled to the *same wages, neither should a stockbroker make more than an engineer who produced products of all kinds.*

Please do not believe the lie that half the country does not pay taxes. It just is not true. They may not pay federal income tax. But they are still paying a large percentage of their disposable income on local taxes.

While Right Wing Media will have you believe most people are lazy, it is not true. Most Americans work extremely hard. The Right seeks examples of stragglers and then try to impose their characters on a false equivalence.

Progressives and most Americans do not want handouts. They do not believe anything is owed to them. They want everyone to have equal access to success. Just like high school is now a baseline, they want the same to apply to college and healthcare.

Countries with much lesser means than us do it. We chose to mislead our population to give a few a tax cut at the expense of an ever-improving society.

You wrote, "The only thing you are owed, is what you earn for yourself." I must completely disagree. I believe I am my brothers' and sisters' keeper. That is why we formed societies. I believe in equal opportunity, equal access to success, but not equal outcomes.

Suffice it to say I did not receive a response. But I think the dialogue was important enough to make a Politics Done Right program out of it. Her belief-set reflects that of many others like her.

Caller receptive to single payer after the call

My radio show Politics Done Right is electric whenever discussing single payer Medicare for All. The subject tackled pharmaceutical companies gouging American citizens. A caller called in to object to the Blog of the Week in which I concluded with the following.

Ultimately the only solution is a single payer / Medicare-for-all system where drug companies are regulated stricter than utility companies. If they find that too restrictive, R&D can be relegated solely to public Universities and manufacture to the lowest bidder.

> *Drug companies sole desire is to make a profit. Humanity plays no role. Why then should anyone believe they will perform any better than a University? Why not pay professors a high salary to develop products based solely on science without the worry of advertising cost, exploitative executives, and shareholders. Single payer gives Americans the power to demand.*

The guest used the standard talking points employed by the pharmaceutical companies and others in the health industry. They claim that absent the high prices American pay; medical breakthroughs would cease. They also claim that foreign countries who have lower prices are sponging off Americans.

The above claims are easily debunked and was made so in a very respectful manner. The caller was receptive to the truth. It is important that we listen respectfully even to those we think are delusional either because of willful ignorance or their preprogramming. I am sure this caller is rethinking his position.

It is important to keep the discussion about improving our health care in the forefront of the national debate. Only then will we be successful in undoing the damage made by those who put profits over humanity. It is the one issue virtually all Americans will have to live through.

Tea Party in Kingwood Area Democrats Tent

The Kingwood Area Democrats were doing what we have always done in the area. We were engaging the community, making early voting a festive event for anyone who approached our booth on the library grounds irrespective of ideology.

It was during the high point of the Tea Party movement. I was friendly with all the Tea Party people as many of them enjoyed the exceedingly long discussions we would have on Conservative vs Liberal vs Progressive vs Tea Party vs Right Wing ideologies.

Most people are averse to overt conflict. My neighborhood is populated with decent civil people of all ideologies that get along but vote very differently with a huge Conservative bias.

That said, you would never hear large political outbursts. Even our Occupy Kingwood was tame compared to Occupy Houston, Occupy Washington, Occupy Providence, and many others I attended.

It is for that reason that the entire Kingwood delegation manning our booth that day were completely in shock when a woman started walking towards the Kingwood Area Democrats shouting at the top of her lungs.

I do not even recall what she was saying. Suffice it to say it offended all the people in our booth, my fellow Democrats and friends. I do not remember if I approached the woman or I was asked to come talk to her when she made it into our space.

To be honest, for me it was the most exciting thing to happen at the booth up to that time. As I approached her it was clear she objected to many of our banners, but the Obamacare banner really got to her.

After shouting down many in the booth she started shouting me down as she was leaving. I remained respectful and civil and asked her to stay and told her I really wanted to understand what about what we stood for so offended her or that she believed was so wrong.

She said she is a doctor and that Obamacare was nothing more than socialism along with the standard tropes. I remained calm as she shouted all her objections. Whenever she would complete a statement eliciting an answer, I would never tell her she was wrong. I simply made her answer her own questions.

When she said Obamacare would bankrupt the nation, I asked her how she would prevent the current system from doing the same. It turns out grouping people to spread the risks is always preferable and larger groups spread it further.

When we spoke subsidies, she said that was too expensive. I asked her if it meant for those unable to get insurance or charity if we should just let them die. That was untenable to her. As she was made to answer the healthcare questions, she calmed down.

Deep inside this woman was not intrinsically a terrible person. Her conservative ideology made her receptive to misinformation from the Republican Leadership, their propaganda network, Fox News, and the Right Wing Think Tanks.

As her answers mimicked Obamacare, -- I never said specifically that she was effectively writing Obamacare with her comments -- she was ultimately making sense. Ultimately when she was using her own mind, doing her own thinking, and not being scripted by a Right-Wing ideology that is not only illogical but senseless, she was onboard. The change was fantastical not only to me but clearly to her.

By the end of the confrontation one would think that she was a new friend. I gave her one of my cards that included the link to my websites and my radio show.

I never expected to hear from her, but I knew the seed was planted. I am sure she has been a visitor to my website.

One must know the limitation of persuasion versus peer pressure. Persuasion that can be coupled with either one's lived reality, the reality they have encountered is long lasting. That is why I do a lot of listening to understand the lived frame of the person I am talking to. I try not to engage until I have a clear picture.

I build the "profile" that I intend to address not on hue, speech, pattern, or ideology, but in the way they think. Why? Because that is the entry point to change. Our engagement must be like that of a virus seeking the best entry point to that which we want to change.

Socialist moniker used as a Right Wink
weapon against progressives

A Progressive caller called into Politics Done
Right seeking advice on how to handle those who
pin the moniker socialist to demonize
Progressives even though the programs
Progressives support benefit all and exist in many
other democratic countries.

My response was necessarily upbeat. Too many go
into a shell the very first time they are called a
socialist. That is the intent. They want the
conversation ended there.

> "First of all I don't think we have to be
> concentrating on the word," I said. "You
> notice I did a show that was titled
> Democratic Socialism and all that kind of
> stuff. And it was just sort of to make it
> par for the course. But in my humble
> opinion I don't want us to be going out
> there just talking socialism using the word
> socialism necessarily because I want
> people to understand what we want to do
> for them. What we want to do for them,
> yeah, a lot of it is going to be what you
> find in Democratic Socialism. But I don't
> want them to have to go look up socialism
> in the dictionary because it is mal defined
> in the dictionary."

I then went on to explain our tenets.

> *"I want them to know if you elect a Democrat, if you elect a progressive right now this is what they're going to be doing for you," I said. "And know what we're going to do for them. We are going to start supporting policies like Medicare for all. Everybody is going to be better off. They're going to have more money in their pockets. They're going to be able to have better vacations. We want to tell them those positive things. Republicans want to sit down and say, socialism Venezuela, socialism Venezuela. They want to make that equation right there. What we want to do is be out there telling people if you elect a progressive this is what you get. And if then they start saying socialism, you say well if you want to call that socialism, I don't care what you call it. You don't fear what people are going to do for you. That's where I want people to be."*

The caller was happy for the response because she thought she had a narrative she could provide in a respectful seed-planting manner. But I reminded her the progressive battle is not solely coming from Republicans or the Right.

"And it's not only Republicans it is some Democrats doing it like I mentioned what happened on Morning Joe" I continued. "The first question they ask. The other day, Chuck Todd was about to go to commercials. Chuck Todd on MSNBC. This is how Chuck Todd went to commercial. 'Well, I'm gonna have to interrupt you guys right now because we have to go to commercials. You know we are capitalist around here.' And I'm sitting down like 'what are you trying to put in people's heads by saying that.' Those are the cues that we're hearing from people. What I was glad to see is that the mayor of New York came on TV recently. De Blasio came on and he really hit it hard when they said are you a capitalist he changed the question to tell them what he stood for and I'm like 'De Blasio that's what I am talking about."

While the GOP is intent on scaring Americans into the fallacy that electing Democrats would effectively be ceding our "great economy" to one that looks like Cuba and Venezuela. Ironically, the U.S. has been instrumental in ensuring those economies get a lot of help in faltering.

One must ask why they do not use Sweden, Norway, or Denmark as the template. They are more representative of the economics system we have in the United States with the exception that they have robust social safety nets.

The reason is clear. If Americans dug too deeply into those countries and studied their economies, it would make their scare tactics ineffective.

Americans would see that an effective integration of our social safety net to our economy is essential. That lends itself to the real development of free enterprise and upward mobility as opposed to a complete unabated corporate control of the country that will ultimately lead to indentured servitude.

If you look at America today, we are not so far from that reality from many who consider themselves middle-class. And that is why so many are in fear and feel helpless.

Recently I read a friend's Facebook post that puts this all into context.

There are 24 hrs in a day.

- *8 hours for sleep.*

- *1 hour for morning prep before work (shower, shave, brush, etc.)*

- *45 minutes to commute to work.*

- *9 hours at work (include 1 hr lunch break)*

- *45 minutes to commute back home*

- *30 minutes to cook dinner.*

- *30 minutes to prep for next work day.*

This potentially leaves you with just 3.5 hours a day to yourself. Most of us use this time to pay bills, do laundry, and rest our bodies after working all day. All this so you can maybe make 40k per year?!?!

* If you have kids, all this goes right out the f*cking window! You literally have no time to yourself, or on quality time with your family. You're literally just packing lunches, cooking, cleaning, and doing homework before bed.

*Not only does American Consumer Capitalism steal your money, it steals precious time you could be spending with the people you love.

What Progressives are fighting for are not Democratic things or Republican things. They are fighting for things to make lives better for us all.

The reason we must open the lines of communication is so we can get that message across. There are powers that must have us at each other's throats to prevent us from realizing that for the most part we all want similar things.

Truth, decency, and morality is on our side. We must not hide from what we stand for even as we talk to those who or oblivious to what we really represent.

Libertarian's fear of government assuaged

This exchange with a Libertarian caller to Politics Done Right illustrates how one finds common ground. It is not by coercion but by the realization that we do in fact share more of the same values than not.

I really enjoyed this dialogue. No one needed to feel like they were abandoning what they stood for.

> "My libertarian conservative point of view is that the government needs to operate in the background like a firewall and stay the hell out of everything else," the Libertarian caller said. "And here's the biggest fear that you're going to have from conservatives and people like me. When the government has control, okay, and it doesn't matter what party somebody starts out at, I find that corruption just seeps into the mix to begin with, okay. When you have a health care system, you know, fostered on you nationwide, my thing is when then does the government get to say, 'Okay, since you're under the banner of the health care system now, we're going to start regulating your diet so you're healthier.'"

I knew exactly where this caller was coming from. My goal then was to mitigate his fears by ensuring he understood that he could be empowered to prevent what he feared most.

"Let me come back really quickly with something," I replied. "Then I have to go to another call. Here is this John. I think we have lost the reality that government is we-the-people. And what I think is if we became civically driven and we started to believe again that we-the-people of the United States are our government, then we would hold government accountable. We would not have to worry about your fears because your fears come from a government gone awry. A government only goes awry because we have allowed as a society the government entities to do so. And how have we done that? By being apathetic. By not engaging our body politic. By allowing us to be a bread and circus community where we get cheap food and we watch reality TV. We care about nothing which leaves a great vacuum for this entity to grow. So, I think one of the things you and I can work together on is to make sure that people get more engaged in government. That way if you are if you really believe you're

> *the government then there's nothing to*
> *fear from the government."*

The caller saw a congruency in our beliefs, and he latched on to it if even with a caveat. That is always progress.

> *"I would agree with that point," the*
> *Libertarian caller replied. "But the*
> *problem right now is I see it as an us-*
> *versus-them mentality."*

I agreed with his caveat.

> *"We need to get rid of that, we really do,"*
> *I replied. "But then I got to go to the other*
> *call my friend."*

I am sure this caller realized that he was being listened to attentively. I was not just preparing a counter argument but first earning his respect by acknowledging his fears. And then ensuring the answer related to what was his real concern.

It was clear that he appreciated the dialogue. While we will not agree on every issue, we knew that agreeing to disagree would not be the end of the dialogue.

Conservative stumble onto show and welcomed the dialogue

A woman stumbled onto my radio show as she channel surfed in her car. After listening for some time, she called in and wanted it known that she is on the Right. Most importantly she concluded what many of us should come to sooner than later. I told her the following.

I started out making it clear I understood we had real differences. But that these differences should not define a human relationship.

> "So, we have to be honest in the debate," I said. "We have to be honest when we start to say these things. I am so happy that you called in as a person on the Right because that is what I want to foment. I want to be able to sit down with somebody on the Right and say. 'Hey, I don't agree with you on this, okay.' In fact, you and I probably have zero agreement on sort of, the kind of ideological issues on religion and all of that. But you know what? It is your business. It's my business."

I then pivoted to economics. Irrespective of religion or anything else. This is shared.

> "But when it comes to economics," I said. "I care about your economic well-being. I

*care about you. I care about your kids
having a good school to go to. I care about
you having good health care. I mean just
as a human being, right? I care about, I
genuinely care about all those things. I do
not care if you're a Christian, a Muslim, an
atheist or whatever. You're a human
being. You have feelings. You have, you
feel pain. You feel hurt. I don't feel good
when I see other people there. You know
what I mean? So, look, anything else you
want to add Janice."*

The caller was engaged and appreciative of the
communication.

*"I just really, honestly," the caller said.
"It's very refreshing to hear this kind of
conversation on air because you don't see
a lot of open conversation between the
Right and Left. It is strictly divided. So,
it's nice to have a conversation to remind
everybody, like you know, we are all in
this together. And, you know, we need to
think back upon like where we stand as far
as hierarchy in as far as well. Because we
aren't there. Those right and left, you
know, whether you vote Republican or
Democrat, you don't have the money so,
you know, think, think."*

I ended the conversation thanking the caller for engaging. I also asked her to inform her sphere of influence about programs like ours. She said she would. If we are conversing civilly, we are fighting each other for a zero-sum-gain.

What ails America should not be frictions between Democrats or Republicans, Conservatives or Progressives, Blacks, Whites, or others, or any of these ideological or demographic differences. It is really a class issue once we mitigate white supremacy which is but a tool by the few to manage the many. Interestingly, the billionaire class seems to want the status quo and centrism and they are willing to pay for it and manufacture false narratives.

As we necessarily drop our guards to lend ourselves to difficult conversations, we often find that they are not difficult at all. More importantly, we feel a new world of experiences and knowledge opening.

Challenge to caller who thinks all immigrants must learn English

While discussing DACA, a Politics Done Right listener called in to complain about immigrants not speaking or wanting to learn English. I challenged the fairness of the accusation.

Many times, one's prejudice is not manifested as a slur or poor treatment. Many times, one uses some other issues that are pretty much a stand-in for said prejudice. This type is much harder to eradicate because it is not easily called out as such.

Here is the reality. One rarely gets a eureka moment when trying to convince another to modify their stance on a specific issue. Changing programmed beliefs and indoctrination occur with patience, It is best when one allows the subject to answer the questions on their own.

Even as the caller agreed with me on mostly all that I said about the original settlers having instituted their own culture and language as opposed to adopting what was already here, he was, in the short term, unable to desist on immigrants learning English.

It was clear from the conversation that like most Americans, the caller was not an inherently bad person. He was made to believe that there was something wrong with an immigrant bringing a piece of their culture. Instead of seeing it as an addition, something to cherish, something to enjoy, he saw it as a threat. He cloaked it in his concern for their economic well-being.

It was obvious that the caller was wedded to his opinion that immigrants must learn to speak English or else. My goal on answering his question was first and foremost to bring up the inconsistency towards the original settlers instituting their language and culture en masse sprinkled with a violent and inhumane treatment of the other versus the attempt to force the new immigrant to conform.

It is ironic because it never seems to upset too many when discussing ethnic neighborhoods like Italian, German, Russian, Hungarian, or others. Why? Because hue to too many is much more significant than one's inherent culture either overtly or otherwise.

Michelle Obama is a born American, descendant of slaves and more American than most. Yet her loyalty to America or right to the White House was contested by many on the Right. Yet, Melania Trump, a naturalized American whose original immigration status is questionable is rarely questioned about loyalty or her right to the White House. It is not at all difficult to understand the underlying dynamics.

The recentness of these types of events are generally good examples to use when asking those on the Right to "enlighten you" as to why one should adopt their positions. Pointing these out in nonconfrontational question form is often effective.

I am convinced that ultimately the conversation with this guy will remain in some remnant of his brain. While he did not immediately change his stance, there will be other cues activated that will help lead the way to his atonement. Most importantly, I am sure many of the thousands listening got a perspective they did not necessarily think of.

A caller said I should never use the term white privilege after the Smollet case

I had a feeling from the beginning of the Jussie Smollett saga that something was off. I never joined the parade because it was clear if this went wrong, its effects would snowball downhill.

Jussie Smollett was an actor on Empire. According to Smollett, he was attacked outside his apartment building by two men in ski masks who called him racial and homophobic slurs and said, "This is MAGA country." He said that they used their hands, feet, and teeth as weapons in the assault.

Smollett was subsequently charged by a grand jury with a class 4 felony for filing a false police report. The next day, he surrendered himself at the Chicago Police Department's Central Booking station.

Soon after all charges filed against Smollett were dropped, with Judge Steven Watkins ordering the public court file sealed. First Assistant State's Attorney Joseph Magats said the office reached a deal with Smollett's defense team in which prosecutors dropped the charges upon Smollett performing 16 hours of community service.

Here is why it turned out worse than I thought. A caller to Politics Done Right used this one incident to discount a real racial justice issue that afflicts people-of-color.

I said the Jussie Smollett name for the first time on one of my shows for a specific purpose. I used his infamy as a call to unite. The goal was to demonstrate a level of privilege afforded few. But most importantly I wanted to show the power of class over everything else.

I reminded the listeners of a form of my favorite phrase; when we unite Appalachia, the Ghettos, and the Barrios, the plutocracy will then fear us. That gives us the real opportunity to get the middle-class-centric policies that we are rightfully demanding.

Divisions across racial, cultural, and other lines are designed to keep us fighting among each other. It forces us to take our eyes off our real oppressors.

Lo and behold the caller used a talking point I knew we would start hearing.

> *"One more thing," the caller said. "Because of what happened with Jussie Smollett, no one at KPFT ever again mention white-male-privilege. It is illegal to mention white-male-privilege. It's called wealthy privilege."*

And there you have it; the privilege afforded a few now-upper-class people-of-color (POC)is supposed to negate a past that afforded more to white people over people-of-color.

Jussie Smollett's privilege must now deny maltreatment by cops that we all see today. It must make us blind to biased care in healthcare, predatory lending practices in the aggregate. And this is just scratching the surface. Sometimes I wonder whether the quiet smile, leading by example, and not complaining too much has served POCs well.

So how did I handle the caller? It was not difficult at all. I gave him several examples.

I was a cyclist in Kingwood for about 12 years or so. We would go on 60 to 75 mile rides every Saturday. Sometimes it would be north of 20 people. But every so often we would go out in small groups. This time it was just two of us doing the long trek.

My friend and I were both dressed in similar cycling gear. Each time I was the first of us to go into the store. Each time the attendant attended to my white friend first. By the second time it was clear to him what was happening. He apologized unnecessarily to me red-faced outside and said, "Now I understand. I understand now."

I also told the caller about my wife being upset with my attire when leaving the house because I would not get the appropriate treatment based on my attire. I went to a hardware store well dressed and a white guy came in looking rough and unkept. Who got immediate service? Suffice it to say my attire meant little in that space. I was able to provide many examples that he could relate to and I am sure on reflection, he had likely seen similar events with his own eyes.

In the end he modified his stance. At no time did I become caustic as I explained scenarios. Ironically, he said his girlfriend is black and have said similar things, so it seems our on-air discussion was validating.

Chapter 6: Informational Essays

There is much we should know about our economic and governmental system that is not always told as it should be. Our schools teach a sanitized version of history.

I write many articles, essays, and blogs daily many times dealing with the immediacy of now. I am also contributing editor to many of our largest progressive websites.

This section consists of or are informed by many of those writings. They provide real world experiences and analysis that should give much of the bases to have productive conversations in a substantive manner with those who you are attempting to open a forward-looking dialogue.

The articles and essays provide a knowledge base that I am sure will be useful. You can read them in any order.

Something more profound is happening to the Right Wing and it is not Fox News

This is a tale of a shocking discussion with a young man, one who is about 19 or 20 years old. It is a disconcerting tale because the young man is brilliant but has been taken in by a terrifying right-wing narrative that will not only endanger the country, but create a permanent underclass relegated to indentured servitude.

If progressives do not find a method and narrative to reach those newly indoctrinated by a corrosive ideology, the demise of our path to an egalitarian society is doomed.

I was sitting in Starbucks, my usual blogging spot, when a young man came and sat next to me. During the prior few weeks, he displayed an interest in appearing on my radio show Politics Done Right to discuss his conservative point of view. I love entertaining different points of view, especially if they are consistent.

Conservatism is not inherently wrong. It is a matter of whether we want to be constrained by the rules of any given ideology. If you want small government and are willing to live in a country where "we the people" render control to the owners of capital, then it is not wrong or right, but simply your preference. Inconsistent positioning, however, is untenable. It is even worse when one builds their position on lies that they fell for via specific methods of indoctrination.

The young man is an extremely hard worker. He does not mind the hard work because he sees it as not taking handouts, with the expectation of self-sufficiency. The man does not realize that his ideological position will relegate him to permanently treading water.

Two scary narratives came out in our discussion. The first is that he believes a high school diploma has become worthless—not because new technology requires a better-trained workforce, but because too many people have it, which makes it useless. He fell for the trick of applying supply and demand to every aspect of life. In fact, he said that when people have less education than a high school diploma, it is more valuable.

The sad part about that argument is that it is partially correct, but wrongheaded. An economy based on unneeded or false scarcity is at best inefficient and at worse immoral (i.e. paying farmers not to grow, or the government buying up overages of cheese, milk, and other products).

The Right is seeking a less-educated populace through its policies. They likely figure they can control the uneducated more easily as automation and robotics make many jobs irrelevant to humans.

The part of his pathology that got to me was the second part of our dialogue. He was very anti-government, desiring that the private sector control mostly everything. I asked him what he thought about oil companies making profits on a substance they did not create. Shouldn't the U.S. Treasury be the beneficiary of most of the gains after they extract the oil? He said no.

I explained that the Treasury getting the excess profits would be for the gain of we, the people. He said he/she who extracts it, owns it. I disagreed but offered a proffer: let the government remove the oil. In that way, under his tenet, "we the people" would own the oil and all profits would go to the Treasury to make the lives of all better, instead of a few. I made him think, but he was not convinced. I closed the conversation by asking him to answer—not right then, but when he went home and slept on it.

If he believes that whoever extracts owns the resource and only those with substantial capital can do so but the government (or we the people) could do the same, why is that a problem? Isn't he giving those wealthy few the inherent right to pilfer us all?

The young man did not have a satisfactory answer but promised he would return with a response. I never heard from him again but I know the seed was planted.

This young man did not learn what we discussed from Fox News. Instead, he mentioned several right-wingers he listens to, some of whom I have never heard of at all. But they are indoctrinating a willing audience.

It takes a lot of work and patience to talk to guys like this young gentleman. But ultimately, it is the only solution in our repertoire.

America is neither Democratic nor a Free Enterprise country. Can we make it so?

The form of government I believe in is true Democracy. The economic system I believe in is Free Enterprise with a robust social safety net. Many get upset when I point out we have neither. Except for what are inalienable rights, in a true Democracy, majority rules.

A majority cannot take away anyone's inalienable rights. But a majority should choose who governs us. And our economic system must be such that one is free to create, build, produce, and sell anything they want if they create no involuntary harm to anyone.

We have a semblance of a Democracy. We are fooled into believing that Capitalism has something to do with Free Enterprise and Democracy. Recall that China is a Capitalist country now.

In a time when 40 million Americans will see suffering not seen since the depression, our economic system is defined by a stock market that is doing comparatively well. One must ask, why? Mom & Pop stores do not trade stocks on the stock market. And as Mom & Pops and small businesses fail, the large corporations and multinationals will grow like no other even with a smaller population capable of spending.

All of this is by design. As this mathematically unsustainable system fails it has to continuously eat parts of itself. And that is you, your assets, your future.

There are answers but we must be willing to dispel our "Powell Manifesto" indoctrination, ideologies, and gullibility. We must be willing to forego our simplistic superfluous rhetoric we as a people have been reduced to as a form of political discourse. Those who control us are not all that smart. They are just more ruthless, immoral, and inhumane.

"Greed is good" as stated by the fictional self-serving Gordon Gecko of the blockbuster movie Wall Street, is false. Reality proves that greed as the motivational factor for a vibrant economy is provably false. Think about how baseless the statement is.

1. The people who invent, create, and serve have been doing so at a discount to those with capital for centuries and they have yet to kill the billionaires out of greed to take the earnings that their intellect and service created. And that, that there is more of those who serve and create than those with capital from a system they have rigged since the inception of America.

2. Capital/money does not have intellect. If you drop 1 billion dollars on a table, it can create nothing. It needs the human with intellect to accomplish something. So yes, the billionaire is useless. Yet, in our economic system, we have given preeminence to capital over people, over humanity.

It is important to note that our economic system creates a façade of a meritocracy. The reality has always been, you must be invited explicitly or implicitly to succeed. When tools are developed to level the playing field, capital eats it again.

Example: Record companies and talent companies used to choose who would become stars. It seemed like the internet would level the field. Talent could go directly to the people via social media and other forms. People got the freedom to choose who they liked, who would excel. Guess what happened? The powers found ways to remove the democratization of the internet by controlling its ubiquity and neutral efficient access. They will have the ability to neuter those who do not play in the form they allow one to exist.

In my book *As I See It: Class Warfare the Only Resort To Right Wing Doom*, I gave examples of how the patent system and other methods are used to limit one's success. Again, America is not a meritocracy.

We have a small window to save our small companies and Mom & Pops and to restore the democratic value of the internet. This is not the time for the Conservative/Liberal/Right Wing/Progressive debate. The masses are on the same team.

Our biggest obstacle is ensuring people are truthfully informed. The thing is, mathematically we can inform quickly. Geometric progression works. But, practically, we must get around the indoctrination and all the isms for the message to seep in, to empower us all to empower ourselves.

I am positive that we will ultimately create the only survivable society, one that is egalitarian.

We must take back our wealth from the
super-rich methodically before it is too late

Many think that when anyone criticizes the super-
rich—specifically the multimillionaires and the
billionaires—that it stems from nothing more than
wealth envy. While that may be true for a few
who themselves were unable to attain that feat,
for most it is about equity and fairness.

Most remember the speech about greed given by
Michael Douglas' character Gordon Gekko in the
1987 movie Wall Street. It was short, but it was a
confirming catalyst that allowed me to see the
fraud that is our current economic system.

> *Teldar Paper, Mr. Cromwell, Teldar Paper
> has 33 different vice presidents each
> earning over 200 thousand dollars a year.
> Now, I have spent the last two months
> analyzing what all these guys do, and I
> still can't figure it out. One thing I do
> know is that our paper company lost 110
> million dollars last year, and I'll bet that
> half of that was spent in all the
> paperwork going back and forth between
> all these vice presidents. The new law of
> evolution in corporate America seems to
> be survival of the unfittest. Well, in my
> book you either do it right or you get
> eliminated. In the last seven deals that*

I've been involved with, there were 2.5 million stockholders who have made a pretax profit of 12 billion dollars. Thank you. I am not a destroyer of companies. I am a liberator of them! The point is, ladies and gentlemen, that greed, for lack of a better word, is good. Greed is right, greed works. Greed clarifies, cuts through, and captures the essence of the evolutionary spirit. Greed, in all of its forms; greed for life, for money, for love, knowledge has marked the upward surge of mankind. And greed, you mark my words, will not only save Teldar Paper, but that other malfunctioning corporation called the USA. Thank you very much.

The essence of that speech was that of a master, a puppeteer, controlling companies and thus the lives of millions via financial transactions that built or created nothing of value. They made money by seeing the economic pieces solely as pawns to play with in a game of wealth extraction. Plutocrats and capitalist apologists can attempt to frame it in a more palatable form, but they cannot remove the stench for those not wearing gas masks.

It is clear, however, that Americans are not greedy to the extent that plutocrats are, and plutocrats, prey on that reality in order to gorge themselves. If greed were good and we all suffered from the excesses of it, the ones who would succeed would be the ones capable of making something of value to society, not those who depend on the manipulation of numbers.

When writing my first book, As I See It: Class Warfare the Only Resort to Right Wing Doom, I exposed my economic innocence and quickly learned how a free enterprise system is supposed to work.

> *When I came to America in 1979 to attend college I had very little knowledge of economics. At 18 I knew nothing about the stock market, taxes, supply, demand, money, or the interactions thereof. As an engineering student, economics was not a part of the curriculum either. As an avid news geek, I remember hearing terms like inflation, stagflation, Dow Jones Average, and all these other economic terms. I wanted to learn.*

> *I decided to take an Economics 101 class. The class was an eye opener. It is there that I learned about supply and demand. I remember one of the first questions the professor asked was what would happen to the price of a product if there was a lot of*

demand for some particular product. In my naivety I said the price of the product would fall since the person or company selling the product would have made enough money to cover expenses and could then afford to lower the price. I just could not help but feel that increasing the price for something that was selling well was ethical. Well I learned fast that the free enterprise system as designed operated differently and that pricing was actually how we maintained a somewhat balance on supply and demand.

If Company "A" has a product, they can increase the price of that product just to the point where its price times its volume less expenses to make the product causes a drop in overall profits for that particular product. A product price that generates a profit will ultimately cause a Company "B", Company "C", and so on to start making a similar product and likely price their product lower than Company "A" in order to appeal to some of Company "A"'s customers. Company "A" will be forced to lower their prices to prevent the other companies from taking all their customers for that product.

The above scenario is known as competition and in a free enterprise system free of corruption it is self-balancing, self-regulating, and efficient. In a free enterprise system, you have the freedom to create virtually any product or service that you believe a demand would exist for. Demand for what you, an entrepreneur has to offer will determine if your product or service would be profitable and profitability of that product or service will likely determine if others are likely to offer similar products and services to compete with you. This is good for our society all around because competition will keep prices of any product or service more affordable while preventing the concentration of accumulated wealth (excessive profits) in the hands of a few. It is a system that when implemented fairly works for all those who want to produce, create, or be entrepreneurial.

I learned about free enterprise but was never indoctrinated by what our business schools try to impart on their students. Capitalism is not free enterprise, and Gekko was not an unrealistic character. We have come to see that today's plutocrats create more damage to the world economy than he ever could. They made an extractive, immoral, pilfering system acceptable.

While still going through the process of learning the real economic system beyond the macroeconomics courses I took, I went to see the Eddie Murphy movie Trading Places. While the movie Wall Street was confirming, Trading Places was the movie that opened my eyes to the fraud of a system where those who produce with their labor and intellect were not the beneficiaries of their worth.

Eddie Murphy's character was a bum on the streets. Two plutocrat brothers made a bet that they could turn an executive into a bum, and a bum into a Wall Street executive. The experiment was successful for the brother who turned Eddie Murphy, the bum, into a stock trading executive.

The movie had a socioeconomic message. But most importantly, it showed how detached the capital markets are from reality. Even though it was just a movie, research shows there is little knowledge of anything substantive needed to be a player in the capital markets. One just needs to be chosen to be a member of the club, and being a member affords one an inordinate amount of control over the lives of millions, thanks to our corporate structure.

The plutocrat brothers in the movie bet one dollar on the experiment and would have destroyed two lives in the process, had Eddie Murphy's character, not exposed the bet. Unfortunately for most Americans, those responsible for discovering the "bets" are willfully asleep at the wheel, and Americans have been paying the price for this for more than 40 years.

No human being has provided enough labor and intellect in our current economy to be worth $100 million, let alone billions of dollars. That hoarding of capital is on the backs of most working people, directly or indirectly

We can do better. We must think outside of the box. But we must begin by recovering the wealth that this system allowed a few to extract from our economy, effectively acting as an economic parasite to most of us.

It will not be easy to get these policies passed, given the number of elected officials on the take. But we must do it.

The democratic leftward move is but the correction of fraud on Americans

Many Americans are buying into the idea that the Democratic Party is moving too far to the left. The thing is movement is relative. Is the party moving left or is the status quo, in reality, edging right? It does not matter.

What exactly does move to the left mean? If one listens to the mainstream media, regardless of slant, just about every policy that is proposed by progressive candidates is a left-wing idea.

It is important to understand what the establishment is doing. It is a psychological ploy. When one categorizes a policy as left-wing before it is even explored, the tendency is to view it through that prism from the beginning.

This is the Democratic Message

So, let us review some policies that are considered left-wing and illustrate why they are not, as we create a narrative that even the conservative rank-and-file should be happy to support.

Student Loan Forgiveness

Progressives see loan forgiveness as stiffing the bankers who have wronged many with burdensome interest rates and fees. They also see it as double-dipping. In effect, Americans invest in their education, giving corporations access to a reduced-cost resource to yield a more substantial profit for their shareholders.

But the conservative narrative is that loan forgiveness is a tax break for those who invested, making themselves more attractive to corporations. We will pay for it with the increased economic activity generated by the new spending power of the forgiven.

A woman's complete control over her body

Progressives believe in true freedom. Men cannot have or carry a child. Why, then, should we even have any say? But most importantly, we know that for a woman (or anyone, for that matter), complete control of their reproductive being is an economic issue. Any demand has a financial impact.

And that leads into the conservative ideology. On every panel that I have served on with folks on the right, the first question they ask when one presents a regulation or social program is how it will impact business. The other thing conservatives hate is unfunded mandates. They want government out of our lives. As such, we should make it clear that their values are satisfied with a "don't-ask-don't-tell" policy. They do not want the government to ask, and women have no interest in telling.

Medicare for All, the Democratic way

Progressives want Medicare for All because it is the humane system that is most compatible with health care as a right. Our values also find massive profiting on the backs of the sick, and on people at a time when they have no real control over choices, very obscene. We also know that our tax dollars fund many of the discoveries for drugs and other advances, yet corporations keep all the profits as they turn those discoveries into products.

But here is the angle for conservatives: Currently, purchasing insurance is a choice, especially since Trump made the mandate irrelevant. Whether one has insurance or not, emergency rooms must service patients. Conservatives purport to abhor freeloading. Since we will fund Medicare for All via taxes, everyone will have skin in the game commensurate with what they can afford. In other words: no freeloaders.

But here is a rationale that is even more powerful. Private insurance companies take away your freedom after you choose the one that will control your healthcare and with that your life. The one that becomes your master. Medicare for all gives you too freedom. The first you remain in control of the choice of doctors and your care. There are no networks, caps, etc. Secondly, it is effectively you, directing your tax dollars.

Family leave and childcare (daycare)

Progressives believe in policies that take care of the home and ensure that everyone has equal access to success. This requires social structures that assist families so that issues like child and elderly care are not an albatross.

Conservatives claim they believe in family values. How better to show that they value families? But most importantly, childcare and family leave ensure that mom and dad have a higher chance of staying employed.

Wealth tax

Progressives understand that unless one is solely responsible for a service or a product, wealth is nothing but what was not paid to those who created and produced said wealth. One could use reductio ad absurdum to show that the wealthy, the ones who work the least, are the real parasites in society. As such, one should have no problems or concerns when it comes to taxing their wealth, their capital. Don't you pay a wealth tax in the form of property taxes on your home, car, and other assets? Why should the wealthy not do their part as well?

I tried but cannot find a conservative spin for this one. So, I will leave it as an exercise for you to complete.

Progressives have a lot of work to do. There is an army of accountants, and others that are ready to use maximal scare tactics to destroy this necessary movement. Throughout this book we discuss a few hazards we must be ready to pre-empt to ensure the success of Medicare for All and other progressive policies we are pushing for—and must have.

Our economic system depends on your path to mediocrity

It is hard to accept. But our economic system is not one where the best succeeds nor is it a meritocracy. The marketing of our system is excellent. It has always been great.

We use phrases such as "We are exceptional." We are the greatest country in the world. And many other phrases I cannot think about right now. What we are is the greatest accumulator of wealth in the world. We market our method of attaining said wealth as benevolent, but if we ever decided to look at our reality, it would be a very different picture.

It is important to note that the overwhelming majority of our citizens are honest people trying to survive. Most people have good hearts, even as we are all to some degree brainwashed by the system created by a select few.

Some Americans treat those who are attempting to get into this country for a better life for themselves and their children like sub humans. Thankfully, many of our citizens understand that the evil emanating from some of our fellow citizens is ill-advised and hypocritical. All non-native Americans are immigrants or descendants of immigrants during and after our nation's formative years. Ironically, our initial settlers came to take the land via plunder, conquest, and murder in the name of the King and the Lord. Those coming today are just seeking a job for a better life.

There has always been a bifurcated hierarchy, one part real and one part imaginary. The latter is the one most of us believe in because we are subliminally encouraged to do so.

The basic issue is whether possessing that big a portion of the pie is deserved or not. I contend that it is undeserved. It isn't about wealth envy. It is about who does the work and who gets rewarded for said work.

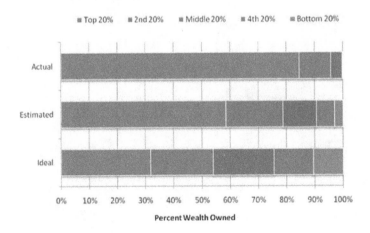

Attribution: Slate

The bar labeled "Actual" is the actual wealth distribution in America. The bar marked "Estimated" is what most Americans believe is our wealth distribution. While Americans understand there is a disparity, they do not know how bad it is.

How much should CEOs earn compared with the average low-skill worker?

Researchers Sorapop Kiatpongsan and Michael I. Norton asked 55,000 people around the world how much they thought CEOs in made compared with the average low-skill factory worker, and how much they should make. Here are the estimated, ideal, and actual ratios. All ratios are to 1, so 93:1, 40:1, etc.

Country	Actual ratio of CEO to worker pay ▼	What subjects thought was the ratio	What subjects said would be the ideal ratio
Poland	28	13.3	5
Austria	36	12	5
Denmark	48	3.7	2
Portugal	53	14	5
Norway	58	4.3	2.3
Japan	67	10	6
Israel	76	7	3.6
United Kingdom	84	13.5	5.3
Sweden	89	4.4	2.2
Australia	93	40	8.3
France	104	24.2	6.7
Czech Republic	110	9.4	4.2
Spain	127	6.7	3
Germany	147	16.7	6.3
Switzerland	148	12.3	5
United States	354	29.6	6.7

Attribution: Slate

The average annualized return on the stock market is about 10%. The average growth rate of the economy is about 2.16%. While there is not a one-to-one correlation between stock appreciation and growth rate, there is an extrapolated reality here. 10% of Americans own 84% of all stocks. If the wealth and income of a small portion of the population are growing much faster than that of the rest of the people, and the economy as a whole is growing much slower than said growth, it means that 10% is enriching itself at the expense of the majority. In other words, they are taking a more substantial portion of the pie.

The defect in our economic system is that capital takes on more importance than actual work and humanity. Policies that give those with capital preferential tax rates because they risk it as opposed to those who risk life and limb are probative.

Recently, Politics Done Right detailed why our economic model is destined to failure for all but the plutocracy and the chosen, its wards, in an episode titled "They designed our economic system to prevent most from achieving & here's why." It made several points.

- Our economic system is not based on pure merit. Instead, it is based on being chosen. In other words, there are many who are qualified, but only a few are chosen. Many

MBAs are just as qualified for any job at banks and investment banking firms, but a select few are chosen based on subjective criteria within the qualified group. This applies from profession to profession.

- Since the '70s, we have had a 400% productivity increase. In that scenario, we should be working 10 hours a week with abundant leisure time.
- The rest of the world was like the heat sink of the internal combustion engine or air conditioner for American capitalism. It afforded a bloated plutocracy, but there was enough for the working class. But to sustain the plutocracy's desired growth rates, the American worker became the final source of extraction. As they reach the level of indentured servitude, the entire system collapses.

For us to make a change, we must first understand the pathology of the masters of the economic system under which we live. After understanding it, we can easily see why the masses will never succeed.

If we are to correct our system, it will mean creating a real free enterprise economic system where those who were not chosen or did not want to be chosen can function within an economy where they can succeed because of an established social safety net (Medicare for All, childcare support, affordable education, etc.).

Protests, Violence, law & Order

What about all the violence and mayhem taking place during the protests in America in 2020? Many are curious because to them it seems like there is no law and order and that could lead the country to a dark place.

Here is the reality. Almost no one supports violence. No one supports hurting human beings. Unfortunately, the converse is not true. As a society, we have learned to kill the human and the human spirit with impunity all to satisfy the few. It is that which keeps order until it breaks when some are triggered enough to react. We are so good at it.

We have a health care system that inherently kills. We have police that are enforcers that use a form of terrorism against black and brown bodies as a check against all Americans. We have an economic system that is tantamount to antiseptic or sanitized slavery.

The genius is that most are unable to see the design when the well-oiled machine is running at a steady state. But as soon as there are disruptions, then the most aggrieved are the first to see the evil within.

The COVID-19 pandemic disruption visited America in 2020. Black people and Latinos in the aggregate are dying at substantially higher numbers because of the confluence of being the ones with the least, the ones who do the jobs that are exposed, and downright medical racism.

We also had a confluence of events that made it clear to many in the majority population that decided not to be willfully ignorant, blind, or both. They saw police, vigilantes, and the system in general as a clear and present danger against POCs. Most importantly, for several reasons they could see that they would not be immune forever as an unsustainable system will eventually have to eat them until its ultimate demise.

Let me make one thing clear. The economic collapse of 2020 is not solely the fault of COVID-19. As I have written before, the REPO market was collapsing during Trump's "great economy" and sustained solely by the Feds manufacturing liquidity for months. His economy was about to collapse.

If anything, while COVID-19 killed the economic well-being of the masses, guess what, the stock market was still being propped up by policy. Again, capital over humanity.

You asked about violence? While I do not condone it, given that our system's sole concern is capital, the threat of endangering their capital, as one can see now, apparently gets more results than asking peacefully decade after decade.

There is no surprise here. When our founding fathers felt aggrieved by England, they did the same thing. When we did not like Noriega facilitating the capitalist notion of providing America with its requested drug supply, Bush bombed the cities of Panama City, Colon, & David, killing 10,000 people to stop it as they brought Noriega to the United States.

So, we should be careful how we describe the reaction from an ignored aggrieved. That said, there are organized Right-Wing rings as pointed out by the FBI doing the most heinous property damage/fires throughout the 2020 protests.

Americans must open their eyes to our reality. A false narrative does not endure forever as reality becomes real. Do not be caught flat-footed.

Middle-Class Must Assert Its Worth to Assure Their Share Of America's Wealth

It is time for the middle class to stop accepting crumbs for their labor and innovation. It is time for the middle class to demand, not ask, for programs that recover ill-gotten gains from a system that by design penalizes work and glorifies capital.

Scientists research a subject or natural phenomenon in detail. Engineers use the body of work and research done by various scientists to come up with useful products for us all. Doctors in partnership with scientists and engineers effect the development of tools and medicines to provide a service, healing. Businesses employ citizens and sell products and services to citizens. Citizens deposit their savings in banks who lend it out to businesses at fair interest rates that allow the banker and staff a good wage and depositors a fair return on their deposits.

The above is a simplistic view of what free enterprise should look like. Purposely left out are two specific professions, teachers (from elementary school teachers to university professors) and the movers of capital (investment bankers, corporate raiders, etc.).

Without a doubt, the most important profession in the world is in fact teaching. All the professions listed above were the result of teachers moving knowledge to the next generation. The movers of capital, however, can only be considered a parasitic venture.

The movers of capital have no interest in what a specific business does. The fact is that because the movers of capital are generally oblivious to science and subservient to the dictates of an assumed efficient capital market, their moves while making money for a few in the short term, generally hurt those it purports to help. The fact that the movers of capital would support businesses cutting employee hours in lieu of providing healthcare is probative.

The movers of capital lack of wisdom and foresight are evident. 40 years after the oil embargo there were no substantive investments in alternative energy even as countries like Brazil had. They have affected a business model heavy on outsourcing to maximize profits at the expense of wages falling locally along with an increase in unemployment.

Lower wages and higher unemployment are tantamount to lower sales which spiral a country into contraction. This ultimately leads to an eventual and certain depression.

The indoctrination by a large percentage of our citizens into believing that only these movers of capital have the wherewithal to create jobs while government cannot, is provably false. It is this false tenet that allows many to believe their unwarranted worth to our society. Small and large businesspeople create jobs. They are worthy of their profits.

Government "we the people" create jobs as well. After-all teachers, police, firefighters, government scientists, engineers, and the like are all real jobs that add to our economy and societal value. A dollar spent whose genesis is the taxpayer receiving a needed service from the government is no different than a dollar spent whose genesis is a taxpayer receiving a needed product or service from a private company.

Sadly, for the movers of capital, it is imperative that the narrative of government not creating jobs metastasize in the American psyche. Only then can they keep unemployment high, wages low, and profits obscene. Is it any wonder they do not want massive infrastructure spending? Too many jobs created will cause wages to go up and profits to be fairer.

The movers of capital have a vested interest in maintaining their façade of worth to society. They must convince us that while the working person must pay up to 39.6% in Federal Income Taxes and up to 12.4%+ in Social Security Taxes that they should pay just a total of 20% (i.e., all pay 2.9% in Medicare taxes). They must convince our citizens that absent the outsourcing, trading, selling, and bankrupting of companies for which they almost always profit immensely, that job creation for said action occurs in the aggregate.

The state of the American economy should dispel this myth. Their goal is never patriotic or noble. It is always to maximize the capital appreciation for a very select few, a privilege most Americans are not privy to.

The reality is the movers of capital have been a detriment to our society. They have used outsourcing and offshoring to keep unemployment high and depress American wages.

They have purchased politicians to stop governmental job creation. They have usurped the religious ideologues to further pilfer the middle class.

The sonogram laws that were passed in several states a few years ago created a big market for sonograms. The decimation of funding for Planned Parenthood will not lower abortions but instead create a demand for higher cost private abortion clinics. State budget lower taxes decimate education budgets as they increase marginally after-tax profits for corporations.

Student forced to finance their education with high-cost private loans further enhances the profits for the movers of capital. Implementation of Voter ID ensures that by the time citizens realize their government has pilfered them; the voter suppression laws make them impotent to vote the culprits out.

Society has been programmed to deem these characters meritorious of the highest incomes and thus worth. Worth in America must be reclaimed. Worth must be commensurate with what one produces for a society that provides intrinsic value. This is not at all difficult to ascertain.

Absent the teacher, education stalls. Absent the engineer, bridges, buildings, & computers are non-existent. Absent the doctors we are unhealed. Absent the scientists we do not have a body of knowledge. Absent the movers of capital, life goes on, and the local banker who has a real interest in the community is reborn.

America's indoctrination by a small class that provides no product or real service to most of our citizens must end. Americans must first visualize and externalize their real worth to society. They must let loose those shackles of indoctrination. The middle class must not accept the current wage or wealth paradigm. The middle class must assert its worth and force politicians to recover the nation's treasure and invest it in America and Americans, those that have done the work and innovation to make this country great.

Progressives: Be careful of the comfort of placating the privileged at the expense of the afflicted

Most Americans are non-confrontational. Ironically, many times they predicate their opinions based on the verbiage of those who are the most vocal. When one polls Americans about their value set, they are decidedly Progressive. They believe in social, criminal, economic, and racial justice as concepts. Why? Because deep down they know it is right and they are able to empathize with abstract concepts.

Interestingly, at times actualizing all those good values Americans believe in, find itself in conflict with reality, history, and individual courage. There are many reasons for that. One primary reason that encompasses them all, however, is the inability of many to empathize unabashedly.

Recently I received very upsetting emails from two friends in a particular organization who want Progressives to temper their speech because it makes some uncomfortable. This discomfort they say detracts from the ability to bring these people into the fold. The question is; if one must tell less than the truth to bring some into the fold, what good is having them in the first place? Is not said lukewarm entry a revelation? A sign of unreliability?

I immediately remembered a quote from a letter Martin Luther King wrote as he spent time in a Birmingham jail. The issue is much more profound today. Replace the words "white moderate" with "some Progressives."

> *I must make two honest confessions to you, my Christian and Jewish brothers. First, I must confess that over the past few years I have been gravely disappointed with the white moderate. I have almost reached the regrettable conclusion that the Negro's great stumbling block in his stride toward freedom is not the White Citizen's Counciler or the Ku Klux Klanner, but the white moderate, who is more devoted to "order" than to justice; who prefers a negative peace which is the absence of tension to a positive peace which is the presence of justice; who constantly says: "I agree with you in the goal you seek, but I cannot agree with your methods of direct action"; who paternalistically believes he can set the timetable for another man's freedom; who lives by a mythical concept of time and who constantly advises the Negro to wait for a "more convenient season." Shallow understanding from people of good will is more frustrating*

than absolute misunderstanding from people of ill will. Lukewarm acceptance is much more bewildering than outright rejection.

I had hoped that the white moderate would understand that law and order exist for the purpose of establishing justice and that when they fail in this purpose they become the dangerously structured dams that block the flow of social progress. I had hoped that the white moderate would understand that the present tension in the South is a necessary phase of the transition from an obnoxious negative peace, in which the Negro passively accepted his unjust plight, to a substantive and positive peace, in which all men will respect the dignity and worth of human personality. Actually, we who engage in nonviolent direct action are not the creators of tension. We merely bring to the surface the hidden tension that is already alive. We bring it out in the open, where it can be seen and dealt with. Like a boil that can never be cured so long as it is covered up but must be opened with all its ugliness to the natural medicines of air and light, injustice must be exposed, with all the tension its exposure creates, to the *light of human conscience and the air of national opinion before it can be cured.*

Letter from Martin Luther King from Birmingham jail

As I sat in Starbucks, my good friend Dr. John Theis, Professor of Government and Director of Lone Star College's Center of Civic Engagement, walked in to grade some final exams. I told him I was writing an article triggered by an email I receive from a friend. After I told him I would include Martin Luther King's quote he provided another one to highlight the point from another side. These quotes further the notions that while one must be civil, there are virtues that one must not cross. The professor gave me the following Barry Goldwater quote. We are not discussing the wisdom of Goldwater's Libertarianism and strict adherence to state rights which are partially used by nationalists to justify their racism.

I would remind you that extremism in the defense of liberty is no vice! And let me remind you also that moderation in the pursuit of justice is no virtue!

Why the beauty of the very system we Republicans are pledged to restore and revitalize, the beauty of this Federal system of ours is in its reconciliation of diversity with unity. We must not see malice in honest differences of opinion, and no matter how great, so long as they are not inconsistent with the pledges we have given to each other in and through our Constitution.

Barry Goldwater quote

Whereas the current crop of Republicans always goes for the jugular, some Progressives always begin their narrative from a stance of compromise. We fear offending the sensibilities of the Right & Center, or we assume that the positions we take, though correct, are unattainable. This hurts us as it is tantamount to abandoning the afflicted, a reason many think elective politics is pointless.

We could learn something from the Right. They know that repeating lies that go unchallenged become truths in the psyches of many. They are unconcerned about offending Progressives.

Unfortunately, too many on the Left cannot be bothered. They have allowed fallacies and stereotypes to metastasize. Imagine if Progressives had a condensed version of Martin Luther King's narrative when the Right gave the false impression of folk lifting themselves up by the bootstraps. If we repeated corresponding truths in a condensed form over and over without the fear of offending the sensibilities of the Centrists and the Right, we would likely be more effective in passing most of the Progressive policies we promote by popular demand. And we would be serving those we purport to support.

Calling Progressive ideas "on the fringe" is a calculated fraud on Americans.

Americans have been indoctrinated into liking or disliking a policy based on some arbitrarily defined fringe. This behavior is solely responsible for an economy that serves a few.

When Democrats lose too often, they are told it is because they are too Progressive or support too many policies that are on the fringe. When they win, they are told that unless they tack to the center, they will lose in the next cycle.

After Democratic big wins 2018, former Ohio Governor John Kasich appeared on Don Lemon's program on CNN. He admitted that Republicans are moving away from Trump and the Republican Party in large numbers. But it is his following statement that should give everyone pause.

"There is also a very big lesson for Democrats," Jon Kasich said. "If you think you are going to win nationally with Medicare for All, the Green New Deal, and all that other stuff, you're not going to win. Because when you look at what happened in 18, and when you look at Beshear and even look at the races in Virginia, where the Democrats have taken the State Senate, you will find those candidates running closer to the middle than on the extremes."

Lemon then asked Kasich if he thought the country was Center Right/Center Left.

"I do. I do," responded Kasich."

"Even with all the rhetoric and all the division we have going on John?" Lemon asked.

"I think Don, you and I, lot of people, we live in a bubble," Kasich replied. "We hear these voices out here whether they are on Twitter, whether they are on television. We hear those voices. But most people are not focused on those kinds of extremes."

Kasich does not live in a bubble at all. All pundits and former politicians trying to temper the 2018 win as some need to tack to the mythical center are doing what many understand well. They are selling out.

Had Democrats lost big in the 2018 elections, the narrative would have been different. It would have been that the Democratic "fringe" represented by Bernie Sanders, Elizabeth Warren, the Squad (Alexandria Ocasio-Cortez, Ilhan Omar, Ayanna Pressley, and Rashida Tlaib) caused Americans to turn away from the Democratic Party.

The thing is, all who are using their social media, reading their print media, and watching and listening to their broadcast media are already well-exposed to the caricature the Right and many in the Democratic Party have made of Progressives, defining them as some Left-Wing fringe.

The Democratic Party saves its ire for the Progressives while the Right projects Progressives onto the entire Democratic Party as the Socialist lunatic fringe.

Of course, most are coming to the realization that it is just a game they are playing. It is a fraud. It is about convincing Americans that the policies that will reverse all the bad things that have happened to them over the last 40+ years are on the fringe, on the Left. As such, they say Americans will not support it. But Americans have been slowly waking up and the polls show it.

Kasich called out two programs as being on the fringe, Medicare for All and The Green New Deal. Others have called out Student loan forgiveness, generous family leave, and childcare subsidies. I fail to see how any one of these policies could be considered on the fringe. Each would improve the personal economies of millions and with that the overall economy.

If Democrats stay focused on their values with a unified message on these policies, they would be unbeatable because, as we have pointed out ad-nauseam, most Americans support these policies. And those who do not are generally in an ideological labyrinth.

Americans know that the soul of the Democratic Party is with Progressive values. And they voted overwhelmingly Democratic in 2017 & 2018.

Democrats should be working on a unified message with the policies we know people want. We must be ready to re-educate away from the tenets of the Powell Memo as well as away from the onslaught coming from the Right and from some who purport to be Democrats.

Let us be clear, a unified Democratic message on Medicare for All sells itself because most have already interfaced with the corrosive nature of private health insurance. If one makes the case Bernie Sanders and Elizabeth Warren continue to make, 'Your healthcare cost will go down and you will have more money in your pocket with better healthcare which means your doctor defines your care and not some private insurance hatchet job hired to deny you coverage in order to enrich a few shareholders and executives." Once the disbelief is overcome it will become a landslide winner.

If Democrats adopted a unified message of the existential nature of the Green New Deal, using the increased fires, floods, destructive storms, and high tide street flooding in coastal areas, it would become a landslide winner.

If Democrats adopted a unified message of student loan forgiveness, by pointing out to Americans that the influx of dollars into the economy from those formerly saddled with an unbearable debt would start buying homes, appliances, cars, and much more.

If Democrats adopted a unified message on childcare and family-leave subsidies showing not only the job creation nature of the policy but the human dignity one gets for being able to have kids while they work or create one's own venture, the policies would pass in landslides.

The lie that there is not enough money to pay for all the above and more is just that, a lie. A few Americans decided to create an economic system that values capital over humanity -- allows a few to hoard the capital created on the backs of others. Adjusting our economic model that values humanity's worth would be transformational for most.

The problem is that unlike the moral wealthy like the Patriotic Millionaires and the likes of Nick

Hanauer, too many of our wealthy enjoy being pathologically selfish, evil, and inhumane Plutocrats. And unfortunately, there are a few politicians in both Parties who are nothing but their wards and by nature of their association, are the conduits for turning the Plutocrats' dollars (read bribes) into narratives and policies that confuse and ultimately drains the wealth of most Americans.

Just run the numbers: Medicare for All is the best option

Examine the realities that our economic system places on our healthcare and more. Absent strong regulations its inhumanity is obvious.

Of course, codifying healthcare as a right where everyone must have access to healthcare would force an economic system to adapt to that reality across the board.

An economic system is not divine. It is human made. If there is a lot of work to be done and services that must be provided, and there are people that are idle and available to do the work, and the excuse for the inability to connect those is that there is no money to do it, then that economic system has failed and must be transformed to one that takes the human realities into account. Insanity is doing the same thing over, and over again and expecting a different result.

The reason we have not adjusted our economic model to our lived reality is that those who profited from the rigged extractive economy designed to benefit a select few would likely lose a substantial amount of their ill-gotten wealth.

Recently a caller to my Pacifica Network KPFT 90.1 FM Houston program "Politics Done Right,"

Syed, said that his name appears on an Affordable Care Act policy. He said the cost is 20% of his income. Even with that reality, he is unable to use the policy because of its high deductible, $6,000. Syed wanted a better understanding and I gave it to him.

The reason people are not rushing to and virtually spilling blood for Medicare for All is that it simply seems too good to be true. But it is not.

All one must do is remember basic math. If one system that administers medical payments require hundreds of duplicate services, equipment, software, & databases, and must make profits for passive investors, and must pay thousands of executives millions of dollars, then it is mathematically impossible for that system to be more efficient than one that must provide the same medical payments without those expenses and overhead.

Not even an inordinate amount of waste and fraud in any single-payer system would likely match the legalized fraud of the private healthcare insurance system. It is simply basic math.

Medicare for All vs Current healthcare system

Table 1. Effects of M4A in 2022

Individual effect of M4A	Cost of individual effect
2022 currently projected personal healthcare spending	$3.859 trillion
+ healthcare utilization increase	+ $435 billion
– provider payment cuts	– $384 billion
– lower prescription drug costs	– $61 billion
= 2022 personal healthcare spending under M4A	= $3.849 trillion
2022 currently projected national health expenditures (NHE)	$4.562 trillion
– decreased personal health spending ($3.859T – $3.849T, per above)	– 10 billion
– administrative cost savings	– $83 billion
= 2022 NHE under M4A	$4.469 trillion
2022 federal share of NHE under M4A	$4.244 trillion
– currently projected federal health subsidies	– $1.709 trillion
= net addition to 2022 federal costs under M4A	= $2.535 trillion

Interestingly, a Koch funded study noted that
Medicare for All would cover all Americans for a
lesser cost than the current private healthcare
system that leaves over 30 million people
uninsured. Yes, it is math. They later tried to
lessen what was the reality of the study's
implications.

I explained to Syed that Medicare For All is not
the free stuff its detractors would have most
believe. Everyone will pay for it with some sort
of a payroll tax. The tax, like the income tax, is
based on how much you make.

Everybody has buy-in to the system. Everyone
has skin in the game. It eliminates free loaders.
All able-bodied people have skin in the game.
Most importantly, the cost for most Americans
will be substantially less not only because of the
inherent efficiency of a single-payer Medicare for
all system, but again, it is indexed to your wages.
And that is a good thing.

The teachers who instilled knowledge in everyone and a banker/broker who provides no product and little service to society in the aggregate will have insurance whose cost would be indexed to their disposable income.

The most important part is that unlike backdoor rationing by private insurance that tells you which drugs you can take, which doctors you are allowed to see, and which medical procedures you can have, it is you via your doctor and agreed-upon standards that make appropriate decisions. If you choose to buy insurance for the unnecessary things Medicare for All does not cover, private insurance will still be there for you to do so.

Understand what is happening here. The Plutocracy via the healthcare industrial complex is trying to create plausible justification to continue their thievery on the American people. It has been this way from the inception of the country.

Syed made a prescient observation about America, slavery, and healthcare that I was compelled to address. He noted that in studying American history, he realized that slave owners had to ensure the health of their slaves while corporations do not.

Sadly, because slaves were no more than the properties of the slave masters, they ensured they had healthcare. After all, a dead slave is not only a loss generator of income but a loss of one's capital.

In an economic system that values capital over humanity, an uninsured minimum wage worker or inexpensive worker is more valuable economically than a slave as they are expendable when ill and does not create a capital loss when dead. Once again, the system wins.

I found the following text at a Stanford University site that should give one pause.

> *No less staunch a pro-slavery writer than Dr. Josiah Mott of Mobile revealed the fragility of paternalistic concerns in his attack on the practice of insuring slaves. As long as the Negro is sound, and worth more than the amount insured, self-interest will prompt the owner to preserve the life of the slave; but, if the slave became unsound and there is little prospect of perfect recovery, the underwriters cannot expect fair play—the insurance money is worth more than a slave, and the latter is regarded rather in the light of a super-annuated horse (Genovese, 1974, p. 520).*

By attaching healthcare insurance to employment, the same pathology that governed the slaveholders' behaviors is displayed by corporations. But theirs is more hideous, efficient, and antiseptic. The pilfer is not always easily discerned.

Until we detach healthcare from the employer and ensure that it is codified as a right, American's access to healthcare will continue to effectively decline. Medicare for All solves all our access to healthcare problems.

There is no benevolence from the Plutocracy attempting to serve us with their brand of healthcare insurance. It has always been a hideous wealth transfer engine directly and indirectly. It is one of the reasons for crippled wages and the inability for most to accumulate wealth. We must open our eyes and once and for all stop allowing them to make us neglect math and reality.

Progressives and Democrats need to stop fearing who we are

A friend of mine introduced me to Jim Rigby, a pastor in Austin, Texas, whom I am extremely impressed with because of his thought process, his compassion, and his clear thinking. When the attacks started on Alexandria Ocasio-Cortez, he made a statement that should resonate with every progressive and Democrat. Rigby wrote,

> *"We liberals need to make damn sure that what most offends us most about Rep. Ocasio-Cortez is not that she is disrespectful and arrogant, but that she is who we pretend to be, but really aren't."*

Americans are progressives

While I think he is right with respect to some people, I think the biggest issue is fear. The fact is that every poll proves that most Americans want the tenets that progressives support, but somehow, we cannot get there.

I continue to sense fear in Progressives and Democrats that is completely uncalled for. Know this, the plutocracy has no problem if Donald Trump or someone like him remains or come into power. It would prefer a more intelligent leader, but it could live with Trump or anyone like him.

The thing is that many Americans are currently so fearful that the plutocracy, the puppeteers, see an opportunity. They know that they can convince those who are paralyzed by the fear of extending a Trump presidency into voting for someone who is acceptable to them by calling them "electable." It is important that we not be fooled by the hoodwink.

> *"We can't choose a candidate we don't believe in just because we are too scared to do anything else," Sen. Elizabeth Warren said it best in the debate. "And we can't ask other people to vote for a candidate we don't believe in. Democrats win when we figure out what is right, and we get out there and fight for it. I am not afraid. And for Democrats to win, you cannot be afraid either."*

Hillary Clinton lost the Electoral College in 2016 by fewer than 80,000 votes combined in Pennsylvania, Wisconsin, and Michigan. But she won the popular vote by almost 3,000,000 votes. Clinton did not do enough campaigning in those states, even as activists urged her campaign to do so. Even with the voter suppression in many of these states, the turnout was almost enough for a big victory all around. But almost is not good enough.

Clinton's Democratic Party platform was decidedly progressive. It was not some swing to the left that lost the election-just some tweaks in a few districts in the respective states.

Why did the Democratic Party narrative of the 2020 election focus on some dubious electability metric? Why were there so many entrants in the Democratic Party primaries even though most had to have known they did not stand a chance of winning? How come most of these characters are center-right?

During both Democratic debates, a slew of center-right candidates attacked the progressives on the stage. More surprisingly, they used right-wing talking points against the Affordable Care Act. It was relentless. The progressives onstage were never deterred. And instead, the attacking men were ultimately politically neutered. It seems like many of these candidates had a purpose: disruption. It was as if they were reading a recent Thomas L. Friedman op-ed.

> *Dear Democrats: This is not complicated! Just nominate a decent, sane person, one committed to reunifying the country and creating more good jobs, a person who can gain the support of the independents, moderate Republicans and suburban women who abandoned Donald Trump in*

the midterms and thus swung the House of Representatives to the Democrats and could do the same for the presidency. And that candidate can win!

But please, spare me the revolution! It can wait. Win the presidency, hold the House and narrow the spread in the Senate, and a lot of good things still can be accomplished. "No," you say, "the left wants a revolution now!" O.K., I'll give the left a revolution now: four more years of Donald Trump.

Friedman got this one wrong. Removing Trump is how the revolution begins. It seems to many that a number of these candidates are promoters of a crippling fear. They continuously attempt to move Progressives to the right.

Michael Moore subsequently appeared on MSNBC and dismissed Friedman. He said that Democrats must go bold.

The fear Democrats experience as they choose whether to elevate a progressive candidate or a center-right candidate is uncalled-for and unnecessary. The American population, and specifically the Democratic population, have been polled and have shown that they are ready for progressive policies such as Medicare for All, pay-it-forward tuition, and much more. One should not fear elevating these candidates and punishing those who are nothing more than the wards of the plutocracy, of the oligarchy.

All executives are not selfish thoughtless beings but victims of Powell Memo indoctrination

When one is privy to close friends of all classes, occupations, education, and social status it is hard during times of flux. Why? It's hard not to see them all as dependent variables in an equation even as some of them genuinely believe that they are solely independent variables.

To be clear, as I have grown more socially aware, I realize that in the social equation each person represents both dependent and independent variables. While we would need a yet unmade supercomputer to compute permutations that decide the direction of society based on these, we can make good guesses based on past behavior relative to policy.

Recently I met with two dear friends for a late dinner, one a retired executive, the other, a current executive. While they are supporters of my activism, they continue to be wedded to our failed economic system They continue to make excuses for it even though we are living through its results. It is no longer just theoretical but is observable in real-time.

After our discussion, the subject was still on the mind of one of my friends. He sent me the following in an email.

> Our government managed Postal Service even gets right wrong. I got impeccable, second to none, 2 day service on some shipments to Dallas area. The lady that helped me asked me to leave a comment but the postal website is either broken or too complicated for me to navigate. I don't have those problems with companies that are governed from within instead of by political appointees.
>
> Two of my brothers were life time postal workers and were very proud of it. They were happy for the job security and the pay was sufficient to cover their needs and with a little extra to provide a few wants and the college tuition for all their children. I know they gave their best as employees because, like me, they were still trying to please my Mom even though she was long passed away.
>
> I feel 100 percent that the postal service should not be privatized. This is because it's top priority should be meeting the needs of the community. Whereas I think corporations are best when allowed to

> *operate as an individual within the community and allowed to succeed or fail and die as long as it operates within governance which should ultimately reflects the needs of the community.*

My friend's email gave me the opportunity for a necessary mini rant.

None of my compatriots will disagree with what you said, I told him. Where we disagree is the delineations; what belongs in the public/government/we-the-people sector and what belongs in the private sector.

Folks like me want private doctors, but health care paid for by one payer, our government, funded by a progressive tax.

We want social services we all pay for progressively. We want to isolate services that should be rights in a civilized society and remove them from the profit motive.

A country with the above policies places all companies on an even level to compete in the private sector, without coercing employees' actions with programs all should have equal access to throughout their lives.

I want a well-regulated free enterprise system in which people earn their income, and not a system in which some profit off the backs of others under bought legislation. In other words, I want a private sector that does not inflict harm (such as the current one, in which an oil company can charge $2.30 for gas because it is the point of maximum profit).

Capitalists succeed in the present system because they have purchased politicians to prevent regulations that protect the air, water, and soil. That system does not take into account externalities that should be reflected in the price of every gallon of gas: the healthcare cost of the person living next to a plant (insurance premiums, copays, and deductibles); the price for deeper water purification to make it potable.

The Pasadena, Texas, area is a cancer alley, but that fact is hushed up because all the local corporations are complicit, from the media to the polluting companies. And who are the enforcers? Executives.

My goal, I told my friend, along with that of many others who have taken on this very, very tedious endeavor is to educate. When you and our friends talk about people not thinking about these things, you are right. The reason is that there has always been a concerted effort to prevent people from learning anything detrimental about a corporation unless what it did is so outrageous that it must be exposed.

It is the subtleties that are killing and impoverishing us because they are slow and methodical. And if we have those who are benefitting just enough to be complicit, it makes the job of those trying to make a difference that much more difficult. But as I tell all millennials and enlightened Boomers and Gen Xers I speak with, the system has not yet come up against those of us that don't mind being knocked down a few times because we intend to win for the masses in the long run.

I was inspired when I read my friend's email with that little crack about not wanting the postal service privatized, and how he spoke about competition. It tells me some of the wards of the plutocracy are not yet lost but can still be turned.

Using stories from real life to make the existential fight for Medicare for All real to all

I had not heard from my friend P for a few weeks. She is a local activist with a seemingly non-activist pedigree. I am not even sure what her stance is on Medicare for All.

I knew the doctors diagnosed P's husband with cancer. But his prognosis was excellent. She had continued working her local pages and kept up with her activism work. But then, suddenly, she sent out a note stating that she needed to turn over her political pages to a new caretaker. A local political operative saw the notice.

> "Egberto, did you know that P is backing down?" he asked.

> "No, but I will contact her right away," I replied. "We can't lose her in this movement."

We met at my local Starbucks, where many in the community keep a conversation going on our body politic with people of every stripe, ideology, and socioeconomic background. She said she had been sick, herself, adding to the difficulties caused by her husband's illness.

And then she said something that made my blood boil. They had diagnosed her husband with bladder cancer, a very curable cancer, especially when caught early, which his was. The doctors had recommended a therapy that did not include the removal of his bladder, which would have forced him into using an external bladder permanently.

A private insurance company wanted him to have his bladder removed. P and her husband had to fight with the insurance company for two months before his needed treatment could begin. That meant two additional months of cancer growth because of the pathetic, immoral, unethical, and pilfering nature of our healthcare system. Her husband ultimately prevailed.

It is easy to refute the false attacks on Medicare for All from those who promote a private healthcare system, given P's experience. They claim excessive wait times, rationing, government control, and more. Well, my friend waited for an excessive amount of time for treatment of a time-sensitive illness. This U.S. healthcare reality does not occur in countries with universal health care and socialized health systems such as the National Health Service (NHS) in the United Kingdom. Attempting to force a purportedly less expensive but poor quality-of-life option is a form of rationing. And having to beg the insurance company to consent to the doctor's recommended treatment is a loss of patient and doctor control.

As we fight for Medicare for All at home, Donald Trump went over to the United Kingdom and told its citizens that U.S. corporate access to the NHS had to be on the table in any trade negotiations. It created a stir in most of the country. The British have no interest in the privatization of their healthcare system. Even as their system is getting more expensive due to an aging population, it is still much cheaper than ours. And their outcomes are better than ours. The pilfering extractive private insurance companies would love to deceive the British people into providing a new cash source with false promises and mathematical impossibilities, supposed better service for less money dedicated to health care as shareholders get dividends and profits. How well is that model working the U.S.?

Medicare for All is going to be a fight. Three sides are bombarding us with fallacies: The Republican leadership; the Democratic establishment; and the health care industry lobbyists, including the Partnership for America's Healthcare Future. One expects the misinformation from the Right and their lobbyists. It is unforgivable for any

Democratic candidate to use the Right's misleading talking points to instill unwarranted fear in the American psyche.

It is true that 180 million Americans will lose their private profit-before-health-care insurance. It is true that taxes will go up for most to cover Medicare for All. Americans are smart. They can hear the truth. There is no doubt that they can do math. We do not need to lie or mislead. The math is not complicated.

Everyone who has an income will be in the game, unlike now, when many subsidize both the indigent and the irresponsible. Likewise, taxes will be income-based, based on what one can afford. It is progressive taxation. Most importantly, because there will be no premiums and virtually no co-pays, in the end, most will have more money in their pockets, including doctors, who will no longer have to fight with insurance companies that are attempting to stiff them.

Medicare for All is just the beginning. Americans must recover what the drug companies have pilfered as well. You, the taxpayer, are most often the primary investors in the initial development of drugs. But none of the profits come back to the Treasury.

Want to control drug costs, ensure that every price increase results in more money coming into the Treasury? Unbridled pricing power is partly responsible for wealth disparity, as those with pricing power over any product or service, can take all your wealth and credit away.

Too many of our politicians have sold us out. We have accepted it because they have high-priced think tanks that create plausible arguments that support the pilfering. It is time to end it.

Kaitlin's story is the kind that we must fight to leave in the past. Just as slavery, with the elite profiting immorally from the work and bodies of others, was evil, so is our healthcare system, as it profits from our bodies and our suffering. It rips us off at times that we are unable to choose, times when we can't fight back.

Kaitlin is an ovarian cancer survivor. She had access to reasonably good insurance through her husband's job. He lost that job, and they are both now without coverage. Recently, she responded emphatically to Democratic primary presidential candidate John Delaney's tweet justifying his attack on Medicare for All.

> **John Delaney Tweet:** "At a minimum, we have to be tolerant of different views on achieving the same goal: universal

healthcare. That's why I responded to @aoc tweet with a debate offer. This isn't about slogans - people's lives are at stake. We need debates and the truth."

Kaitlin Tweet: "My life is at stake you asshole. I'm currently not insured because I can't afford it but I'm an ovarian cancer survivor and am supposed to be getting tests and screenings every 3 months. #MedicareForAll"

What Kaitlin is living through is but a hypothetical to many of these candidates who are on the dole either from us or, who knows, future kickbacks for allowing the continuance of a corrupt system? Kaitlin's story in her own words is piercing, not only for every woman, but for anyone who has experienced the pilfering nature of our healthcare system. My wife's and my own healthcare stories, and those of so many others, follow this pattern. The health-industrial complex is using its pricing power to legally rob us.

The most efficient method of payment for health care is a single-payer Medicare-for-All system. That is a mathematical certainty. The purpose of any deviation from that system is to make a profit where no profit should be made.

Our economy is large enough to provide earnings in legitimate areas of business and commerce. Profiting off the misery and illness of others requires an indoctrination that we would do well to eliminate sooner rather than later.

Bankruptcy, poor quality of life, the inability to accumulate wealth, and, ultimately, death are the outcomes of our current corrupt system. Wake up, and help others do the same.

Understanding the connecting thread in these race stories, one white, one POC, is important.

My Facebook feed is a bastion of solid writing from friends whose stories often touch me profoundly. Many of them are great at storytelling. Most importantly, many of their stories have immediate relevancy.

This friend's story hit awfully close to home. She wrote the following.

> "This is what NOT having #whiteprivilege feels like. This is the reality of being a POC in America today:
>
> The storms tripped our alarm last night and scared the bejeezus out of us. After [my husband] and I cleared all the rooms/closets/cabinets in the house, we tried to cancel the alarm, but the deputy had already been dispatched. The first thing that came to mind was: WE'RE MEXICAN!
>
> Before the officer arrived, [my husband] and I had our ID's in our hands to prove that we were, actually, the homeowners. The Deputy was friendly, professional, and immediately put our minds at ease. She did a walk through the house and checked

the garage, as well. She even took a moment to admire Ben's whitetail trophies.

After she left and we sighed with relief, I wondered: Do white people feel the need to prove they live in their own homes when an alarm is tripped? Do white peoples' hearts race in fear when they potentially interact with police--in their own homes? Will black and brown people ever stop feeling this way?

Fortunately, we were safe, the Deputy was wonderful, and all is well that ends well. Have a great Monday, peeps! Be safe out there."

I thanked my friend for writing the post because the reality is POCs usually suffer these indignities in silence and if the event turns bad, being followed in a store, being disrespected or worse, most times we just let it pass. I told her it was sad we still have to teach our kids about these survival techniques and that I remember how hard it was to have "THE TALK" with my daughter. Her response saddened me as I remembered my daughter's reaction. My friend simply replied:

> "The Talk" is the worst. Especially when
> they've grown up in the Kingwood bubble
> and think they're immune."

As I told this story on air at KPFT 90.1 Houston on
Politics Done Right, I recounted my experience
with a #DrivingWhileBlack incident.

> "The cop pulled in behind me. Damn. It is
> me. "Move into the next parking lot," The
> officer said through the loudspeaker. It
> was one of those very dark empty parking
> lots off of Westheimer. Now, will this be
> my DWB (driving while Black) moment
> with an 'accidental' trigger happy cop? My
> car has all kinds of Liberal stickers on it
> and also an Obamacare sticker. What kind
> of attitude will the cop have?

> I tried to stay as close to the main street
> as possible. It is a shame that I did not
> know what I did but had a palpable fear
> that actually surprised me. I rolled down
> my windows and kept both hands on the
> top of the steering wheel. I could see the
> officer approaching my car with a bright
> flashlight from the back-driver's side very
> cautiously.

> He then shined the light inside the car and
> then on my sticker.

"Do you know why I stopped you sir?" the officer asked.

"No sir I do not," I responded.

"You crossed over two lanes," the officer said.

"I did not even realize that sir," I responded.

"May I have your license and insurance please," the officer asked.

"My license is in my wallet in my back pocket. Is it OK to take my right-hand off the wheel and get the license, sir?" I asked.

"Yes sir," the officer responded with a slight smile.

I was feeling a bit less apprehensive. This officer was displaying professionalism and respect I had seldom received from any police officer. The officer walked back to the patrol car and stayed there for about 10 minutes. I got a bit concerned. I hope the computer system was not screwing my data up with some felon or something that would then change things. The officer came back to my car.

"I am just going to give you a warning sir. Please note that you gave me an expired insurance card, but I checked, and your insurance is up to date," the officer said. "Please make sure to keep an updated version."

I was so impressed with this cop, I talked him into a selfie. The blog post was exceedingly popular. His commanding officer called me and told me he received a citizen commendation.

These were two incidents that really should not have been anything special requiring some sort of inordinate acknowledgment. But for POCs it is profound.

Ironically, around the same time, I am reading my friend's Facebook post, I hear about Kyle Kashuv.

> *"Kashuv is a recent graduate of Marjory Stoneman Douglas High School in Parkland, Florida. A survivor of the 2018 shooting at the school, he became famous for opposing gun control measures after the attack. Kashuv became the high school outreach director for the conservative group Turning Point USA and lobbied in favor of a federal "school safety" bill that attempts to address the school shooting problem without gun control. He currently*

has more than 300,000 followers on Twitter."

These extracurriculars, together with good grades and high SAT scores, earned Kashuv admission to Harvard earlier this year. But in late May, a series of offensive comments he made roughly two years ago — the repeated use of the n-word in private chats and Google Docs — came to light. Harvard initiated a formal review of Kashuv's admission, and on Monday morning, Kashuv tweeted out a letter from the university formally rescinding his admission."

His Twitter thread where he apologized to the University went viral.

It is understandable for Kyle Kashuv's to fight for his position at the University. The problem is that Kashuv was offensive to both black people and Jews using racial slurs and stereotypes and threatening violence. The University has not readmitted him.

What was disconcerting was to see how many talking heads including MSNBC's Stephanie Ruhle attempting to use the age mistake as some sort of immediate rehabilitation. They seem to want this young man to get a break since he was young.

Did these same people take Michael Brown's age into account or did they just assume he was a thug to be treated like a criminal adult? Trayvon Martin, Philando Castile, Levar Jones, John Crawford III, Eric Garner, and others prove that for POCs, innocence many times is not enough while many go through hoops to protect, defend, and rehabilitate similar behavior in men from the majority population.

If one wants to understand the connecting thread between race and privilege, consider Barack Obama and Donald Trump. I will end with a question. Had Obama fathered children with three different women, grope women, sprout out obscenities in public, displayed a speech/language deficiency, told verifiable lies, use the presidency as a means to enrich, lost the popular vote, and committed fraud in the past on the people he now serves, would he win the presidency, let alone have the media and government treat him respectably or have Congress vacillate on whether to impeach him?

Our Political Mess A Result of False Equivalencies

It is likely that the political stalemate between Republicans and Democrats will be resolved in some manner sooner rather than later. It could have been much sooner than later. The reality is it need not have occurred in the first place.

False Equivalencies

Why did it occur? A media and the political system allowed false equivalencies to rule the day. False equivalencies give plausibility to each side even if one side is provably wrong. False equivalencies encourage the one that misleads to maintain the status quo in their narrative.

Anthony Weiner was creepy for showing his private parts on Twitter. David Vitter using the services of prostitutes broke the law. The media treated these two events as equivalent.

Over the years the GOP has been successfully using a trick that works almost all the times. They accuse the media of having a Liberal bias. They tell their base that the media and institutions of learning are Liberal biased. In doing so attacks on them by the media is perceived by their base as a false liberal attack.

More importantly, however, is what the accusation of a Liberal biased media does to the traditional media. It forces them to overcompensate in their attempt to seem balanced. Throughout the past government shutdown and budget crisis, the traditional media have been attempting to make it look as if it was a simple dispute between two parties that bore the same responsibility. They reminded America that Senator Obama voted against raising the debt ceiling. While true, President Obama's political vote never placed the country in danger.

During the health care debate, the traditional media made it seem like death panels, government takeover of health care, and throwing grandma over the cliff was an equivalent argument to the Democrats arguments for the Affordable Care Act, Obamacare. Inasmuch as these were patently false, giving them equivalent weight in discussions gave the less informed American a 'traditional-media-made' plausible reason to accept a fallacy.

During the President's second attempt at infrastructure-based stimulus, Republicans balked. Even while the country was in crisis, the traditional media did not point out that Republicans have always supported this type of spending. They made it look like a simple disagreement.

Wolff Blitzer went out of character and praised President Obama by saying he has 'Golda Meir Instincts'. A few days later fearing a lack of false balance he jumped into policy and stated Obamacare should have been delayed.

Both parties use the traditional media in an attempt to get some advantage. When issues or a matter of ideology it is the traditional media's role to allow each side to make their point in winning over citizens. The problem is when politicians or their operatives blatantly lie to attempt to get their point across. In that case, the media's role is not to be balanced; it is to inform the citizens of the lies and misinformation. Promotion of false equivalencies should have no role.

It is fair to give balance to the big government or small government debate. Democrats prefer big government (a strong safety net) while Republicans prefer small government. This is a choice Americans must make. Neither is wrong or right. Americans must, however, be allowed to make that decision based on truths.

False Equivalencies stops the debate.

What does big government mean for social security, Medicare, healthcare, parks etc.? What does a system where services are doled out mostly by the private sector mean? These are profound questions that Americans must know. Cloaking the debate in false equivalencies hurts all sides.

If a Republican says reducing taxes and reducing the deficit will have no negative impacts on the social safety net and a Democrat says it will, it is the media's role to give context. They should, especially if there is a history that can be used to evaluate the veracity of claims.

There is no equivalence in most of the political arguments today. The Republican Party has provably lied to the American population, not on their ideology but what their ideology would do to the standard of living of the working middle class. Making their arguments equivalent to those of the Democrats confused Americans just like snake oil salesmen of the past did. This allowed Republicans to get away with a level of lies and misinformation that emboldened them.

It took a government shutdown in a poor economy to show Americans that Republicans were full of it. They realized that they wanted the government much more than they thought. It took the opening of the healthcare exchanges for Americans to start seeing that Republicans were lying all along about Obamacare pricing, affordability, benefits. Republican poll numbers have crashed as Obamacare numbers rebound.

It was not necessary for Americans to have had to take the pain of a shutdown. This was a problem created to extort. If the traditional media had held politicians accountable, Americans would have made the right decisions. No party would believe they could take a country hostage and not pay a political price.

The polls reflect that Americans are paying attention. It reflects that they are holding those that extort, accountable. Even as the traditional media continues to attempt to promote false equivalencies, Americans have gone beyond being led by the media.

Granny's ordeal: Dealing with an inhumane healthcare system

Have you been to a hospital complex lately? In Houston, they are constantly building them or upgrading them. They are beautiful. But the healthcare they provide sucks your wealth and our tax dollars. It is an evil enterprise. And here is why.

I owned a software development company. I have always carried my own private insurance with extremely high deductibles, co-pays, and premiums. I could afford it then but understood why a large portion of Americans not getting employer healthcare had to go without.

If I added all the premiums I've paid over the years, I have paid out many times more than I received in services. Theoretically, that is okay. In pure insurance parlance, they bet you will not get sick enough to be a risk to them and you bet the converse. And if you lose you win because you are marginally healthy at least.

Our economic system attempts to make everything a product. The thing is, most products are real choices. Basic healthcare isn't. You break a leg; you cannot easily shop around. You get cancer, in a humane system, you would not forego care because you cannot afford it. In fact, that statement alone is immoral. It degrades into an ability to pay else suffering and/or death. An economic system in a civilized society should be based on everyone having basic healthcare as a part of said system. Roads are not an afterthought. They are necessary for a functioning society. We have a tendency to have an economic system that reveres capital and penalizes humanity. This touches everyone if they live a full life in the long run.

It was about 1:30 PM on Christmas day. All of our family started arriving for our 2:00 PM meal. Linda, my wife, set the time. Everyone knows whether you are present or not, dinner service will begin. This Christmas would be different, and it is life changing.

While taking a shower, Linda ran into the bathroom. "My mother is not talking, and her mouth is twisted to one side," she said. "I am calling 9-1-1."

Granny was sitting on the couch catatonic. By the time I got to the room, my daughter who was home for her break -- she is a 3rd-year med student -- was already doing pupil dilation tests and some other stuff. She looked at me with grave concern.

"Yes dad," she said. "It is a stroke. A bad one."

Linda was helping Granny up the stairs the night before and her right knee gave out. She said she felt dizzy. We took her to the emergency room, they did some tests, gave her Tylenol, and sent her back home even though she could hardly walk. On the morning of the day of the stroke, she felt somewhat better, but my daughter said the stroke was likely in progress from the night before and likely may have been caught before it got as bad. My mother-in-law's Medicare is handled by WellCare, a private company. It is clear, the intent of the hospital was to do as little as possible. Does profit maximization at the expense of the patient come to mind?

The most sickening portion of the incident occurred when the paramedics got to the house. The first thing they did before even touching her was to ask about insurance. We told them she was on Medicare. They wanted to see the card. My wife was a bit frazzled and could not find the card in granny's purse. They acted like they would not load her in the ambulance given the manner in which he said he needed the card. When Linda gave them the card, they loaded her up and they were off to the hospital.

Granny had a procedure that went through her groin into her brain to extract the blood clot. He showed us before and after blood flow pictures.

Granny is responsive, smiles, and seems to understand, but cannot speak, swallow, or stand. The hospital says that is all they can do and that the family must get her out of there and into a facility.

Granny is on Social Security (very small check as she had low paying jobs), Medicare via WellCare, and no kind of senior care insurance. She could not afford it. It is then one realizes how evil, immoral, and flawed our system is for those who least can afford healthcare.

Medicare will provide living services for a few months and rehabilitation for a few weeks. For all practical purposes after that, you are on your own on the order of several thousand dollars a month. It is a process that means you must give any accumulated wealth you have acquired over your lifetime to these profit centers masquerading as healthcare delivery services. Then and only then does one qualify for Medicaid, after destitution. They act as those cleanup parasites designed to take all the accumulated wealth. And then you die with nothing to pass along.

This system only survives because at any given time enough voters are not experiencing this pilfering. Every politician who has a high school education must understand this. Yet they have allowed their wealthy benefactors to lead the debate on a humane system that prevents this economic and emotional carnage.

My experience owning a business, the ordeal we are going through with granny, the thousands that die every year from the inability to access healthcare whether one has insurance or not demands Medicare for All. The biggest lie is that we cannot afford it. And for those who believe there is security in private insurance or employer-based insurance, remember that Cigna other health insurance companies put the healthcare of over 200 thousand Houstonians at risk negotiating contracts.

My wife and her brothers and sisters struggled to decide how they would move forward with an expense they did not expect. I see the pain and worry. We must all activate our empathy gene. Our system's promotion of a false individualism is in contempt with our empathetic self. This is by design for if we envision our system based on looking through the eyes of our fellow brothers and sisters we would pass policies that mitigate likely the evilest healthcare system in the world. We may have the best technology that fewer and fewer people will have the ability to access.

My mother-in-law died on January 8th, 2020. Her last few days saw suffering no human should endure. But she is at peace now.

Sadly, I watched a private healthcare system pilfering Medicare for all that it could get away with within the short time between her stroke and her death. Of course, it is no different than what the private health care industrial complex does to us all.

Most doctors, nurses, and participants are wonderful people trained to rip us all off to enrich the few owners and shareholders. I learned a lot more about the degeneracy of our system.

Vote in politicians that are willing to make the transformational changes we need for most of us. And let's make sure those who have adopted policies and talking points that harm are summarily dismissed.

New form of slavery not racial but subtle.
more dangerous & affects all

Slavery based on the color of one's skin or ethnicity is horrendous. However, there is a new form of slavery. It does not come with a whip. It does not come necessarily with physical scars. It is subtle but more dangerous because we ultimately choose our enslavement to the corporation.

But the new kind of slavery can be mitigated if one enters into corporate servitude with eyes wide open with an independent exit strategy. In other words, while the corporation's fiduciary responsibility is to the shareholders and not the employees or customers, one's loyalty should be to self, relative to the corporation.

I realize the words and encouragement I received from my father were more profound after leaving my software company to become a full-time political activist more so than after abandoning the corporation I worked for to start what turned out to be a very successful software development company. Why? Because I was able to study the corporate pathology that causes voluntary enslavement.

After deciding to leave corporate America to start my software company, some in my family were not thrilled. My father's words were simple but ultimately profound. "You do all da work," he said with his Panamanian/Caribbean accent. "And they make all the money. You can do it on your own." He also reminded everyone that one could get fired at any time and if I were not darn good at what I did, the opportunities that I made would not have come to fruition as quickly as they did."

In that one interchange, as simple as it may seem to many, he touched on some critical concepts without calling them by name, stealing one's excess labor, intellect, loyalty, and freedom. Whether you work for, intend to work for, or plan to quit the corporation, one should understand these.

One must understand that a corporation was not designed to like or dislike people. Legally, as an entity, it has many rights that supersede that of humans (e.g., Citizens United v FEC). Its sole purpose is to make money at all cost. It is the fiduciary responsibility of corporate executives to maximize the profits of the shareholders and implicitly that of their class for good measure. One is hired into any corporation solely to affect that reality.

One's voluntary enslavement begins with several types of coercions: benefits, and money. These give the semblance of equity. But the power within the relationship lies with the corporation.

The corporation can fire the employee at any time. While it is true that one could quit at any time, most are up against a financial reality or healthcare reality that keeps them pinned to the job.

Moreover, you are either forced to work above and beyond what should be required either implicitly or explicitly. I read an article recently from a document factory titled "7 Signs that indicate you have become a corporate slave" that puts it into context.

7 Signs that you may have become a Corporate Slave

1. You sleep less than an average of 6 hours every night.
2. Part of your daily routine involves turning the floor lights on, when you arrive, and off, when you leave.
3. You have never attended your daughter's dance recital.
4. You can't remember the last time you had a day off, let alone a vacation with your family.

5. You are constantly anxious about your performance, or rather the way it is perceived by your manager.
6. You feel you cannot talk to your manager, your HR or your colleagues about your grievances.
7. Your work-life balance has taken a nose dive.

If all or even any of the above sound familiar, then you might just be in the company of the un-free. On a closer inspection you may actually see yourself among thousands of employees steering the metaphorical ship of your company, chained to the massive oars, much like the galley slaves of the ancient times. Have employers really become the, less gruesome, less morbid, less reprehensible versions of the last century plantation owners?

Of course, they have. It is now antiseptic. It has the semblance of class. The chains are no longer iron but electrical impulses undulating in one's mind cauterizing the thinking process

Why aren't corporate profits shared? If a corporation has total sales of $10 billion and total expenses of $8 billion, then that $2 billion profit is the excess labor of all the employees. Why aren't they getting a cut of it?

Corporate defenders will say that the shareholders put their capital at risk. That is hogwash. Workers put their bodies and many times their health at risk. They put their relationships at risk. And many times, the children are shortchanged irreparably.

Others will ask if workers will share in the losses. Well, they already do with the loss of their jobs, security, and many times pay and more. Ironically, when corporations lose money their stock price may drop but it requires no outlays from the shareholder.

The slow death of the unions, unlimited money in politics (McCutcheon vs FEC, Citizen United vs FEC), deregulation, automation, and global treaties all reduced the leverage and bargaining power of the rank and file employee. We must take control first of our government and pass laws to get money out of politics. We should make unions a requirement to do business. And we must pass an amendment that makes Citizen United and McCutcheon moot.

The above is not wishful thinking. If activists and workers alike work methodically, consistently across election cycles, one can accomplish these and more.

We must come to the realization that the economic system is not divine. It is human made. A few men created it with a particular unequal bias that enriches a few which will ultimately culminate into indentured servitude for the many. And we have been living under it for several hundred years now. It is time for the masses to enjoy what they built.

Marijuana, opioids, & alcohol: It is time to change the paradigm

America needs a paradigm shift in the manner it deals with products that affect our moods, psyche, and our overall well-being. We must do so based on data instead of ideology. Deprogramming many will be difficult. But marijuana must be decriminalized in its entirety.

A Houston cannabis activist appeared on Politics Done Right to bring awareness to many issues about marijuana aka weed aka cannabis. Her goal was first to dispel the notion that there are any valid reasons why marijuana is illegal. And secondly, to activate Americans both locally and throughout the country. As one listens to all the arguments and discourse about marijuana, there can only be one conclusion. The product should not be illegal.

Here are some interesting facts about alcohol.

- 2,000+ Americans die every year from alcohol poisoning.
- 1.4 million alcohol-related acts of violence are committed each year.
- Nearly 10,000 people are killed annually on U.S. Roadways for alcohol-related accidents.

- Alcohol is involved in more homicides across the United States compared to other substances, like heroin and cocaine. In fact, about 40 percent of convicted murderers had used alcohol before or during the crime.
- An estimated 37 percent of sexual assaults and rapes are committed by offenders who were under the influence of alcohol.
- Roughly four in ten child abusers have admitted to being under the influence of alcohol during the time of the offense.

Here are interesting facts about opioids.

- Roughly 21 to 29 percent of patients prescribed opioids for chronic pain misuse them.
- Between 8 and 12 percent develop an opioid use disorder.
- An estimated 4 to 6 percent who misuse prescription opioids transition to heroin.
- About 80 percent of people who use heroin first misused prescription opioids.
- Opioid overdoses increased 30 percent from July 2016 through September 2017 in 52 areas in 45 states.
- The Midwestern region saw opioid overdoses increase 70 percent from July 2016 through September 2017.

- Opioid overdoses in large cities increased by 54 percent in 16 states

And the facts on marijuana.

- There are no recorded instances of anyone dying from a fatal dose of marijuana alone.
- The first, conducted by the Insurance Institute for Highway Safety, analyzed insurance claims for vehicle collisions filed between January 2012 and October 2016. The IIHS researchers compared claims in states that had recently legalized marijuana (Colorado, Washington, and Oregon) with claims in similar neighboring states that hadn't.
- They found that over that time period, collisions claim frequencies in the states that had legalized marijuana were about 3 percent higher than would have been anticipated without legalization. The researchers characterized that number as small, but significant.
- A second study, published in the American Journal of Public Health (AJPH), that found no increase in vehicle crash fatalities in Colorado and Washington, relative to similar states, after legalization.

Reliable data that associated violent crime to marijuana was hard to come by because even government studies tended to tie cannabis use with alcohol. What is clear is that marijuana legalization did cut violent crimes in implementing states.

Alcohol is legal and virtually unregulated. Opioids are legal and regulated. Marijuana is illegal mostly everywhere. It is clear that of the three substances, marijuana is the least dangerous.

The question then is why is it that weed is illegal? One cannot help but make calculated assumptions.

Laws on marijuana are changing all the time all over the world. So much so, people struggle to keep up to date with the latest news. Have a look at Marijuana101.Org to keep in the loop with the latest news.

Can you imagine what would happen if marijuana were immediately decriminalized nationally? The results from the states that have done it are a net positive. That said, it is easy to see several forces colluding to keep the clamps on keeping marijuana illegal.

Counties would make less money in penalties and fines. They like to tote low taxes as they use draconian law enforcement to make up revenue that should be made from taxes.

The prison industrial complex would lose quite a bit of business. It is not only that they would lose those convicted of marijuana offenses, but as the herb is legalized, the reduced violence means that other associated crimes are reduced as well. That means less incarceration.

Most importantly, however, drug companies would likely lose big. Why? There are many ailments where marijuana in one of its many forms may be preferable. As all the proven uses of marijuana go mainstream it cannot help but impact pharmaceutical companies' bottom line.

Anyone who doubts that those realities are not in the back of the minds of the politicians does not understand how the country works. Thousands of lives have been destroyed by ridiculous marijuana laws. Because many value money and ideology over humanity, thousands more lives are likely to be destroyed before real change comes. It is up to us to enlighten others to force the change.

Chapter 7: Conclusion

The polarization in America is particularly useful to a distinct few. It is not natural. It is manufactured by a system whose survival depends on it.

Interestingly, the Founding Fathers had discussions on problems that factions could present when polarization occurred. The following words from Federalist 10 is probative.

> By a faction, I understand a number of citizens, whether amounting to a majority or a minority of the whole, who are united and actuated by some common impulse of passion, or of interest, adverse to the rights of other citizens, or to the permanent and aggregate interests of the community.

> There are two methods of curing the mischiefs of faction: the one, by removing its causes; the other, by controlling its effects.

> There are again two methods of removing the causes of faction: the one, by destroying the liberty which is essential to its existence; the other, by giving to every citizen the same opinions, the same passions, and the same interests.

It could never be more truly said than of the first remedy, that it was worse than the disease. Liberty is to faction what air is to fire, an aliment without which it instantly expires. But it could not be less folly to abolish liberty, which is essential to political life, because it nourishes faction, than it would be to wish the annihilation of air, which is essential to animal life, because it imparts to fire its destructive agency.

The second expedient is as impracticable as the first would be unwise. As long as the reason of man continues fallible, and he is at liberty to exercise it, different opinions will be formed. As long as the connection subsists between his reason and his self-love, his opinions and his passions will have a reciprocal influence on each other; and the former will be objects to which the latter will attach themselves.

I took a class on Federalist 10 with a friend who is a professor at a local college. It was clear that true democracy was feared because factions were free to form. If they are destructive and polarizing as we have today between the Right and the Left, it can put the nation's existence in trouble.

But as explained, removing democracy was not a viable option. Interestingly the second option for controlling destructive factions *"giving to every citizen the same opinions, the same passions, and the same interests"* seemed to be discounted. The thing is, that is exactly what I am counting on to bring us together.

Most of us have the same basic wants, and needs. We all want good healthcare, good wages, child support that allows us gainful employment, the ability to get a good education, a clean environment, a few weeks off a year, and a workweek that is not overburdensome.

What is also true is that those who control our economic system have little interest in modifying the economic system to afford us those wants. Providing these humane services means that those who control our economy will have to justifiably do with much less. After-all, it is the masses who provide the services, the intellect, and the purchasing power that enriches the few.

They create factions (polarization) by creating false differences to encourage fights among people where there should be none. If there is distrust among groups, it is hard to start an honest dialogue.

Again, today's factions are not natural. They are manufactured. When we take off our blinders through dialogue it will become readily evident.

As a Progressive I have convinced myself of several points that allows me to engage the Right fearlessly with humility, civility, and respect.

1. I assume most people irrespective of ideology or inherently good.
2. I give everyone the benefit of the doubt initially.
3. I listen intently and intentionally. And I make the person that I am trying to engage fully aware that I am not just hearing and waiting to respond but that I am really listening.
4. I am more interested in that person voting in their own interest than for them breaking out as a converted person. I am not trying to change someone's party, culture, or religion.

So how do you talk to someone on the Right or to anyone who you know does not necessarily differ from you in your wants and needs; and that is most.

Again, these words; patience, humility, listen, thick skin, selflessness, and genuine compassion.

Chapter 8: Acknowledgements

I dedicate this book to my daughter Ashley Willies, the supporters/subscribers/donors of Politics Done Right (Willies Media LLC), and to every activist out there sacrificing to make a better America. There are wonderful and great people out there.

My daughter Ashley Willies is getting ready to enter her fourth year in Medical School. 2020 has been an ordeal for most but for her it began as a nightmare.

Ashley came home for Christmas as she does every year. On Christmas Day her grandmother got a stroke. Ashley, using the medical skills she had acquired thus far did the stroke validating tests as the paramedics were on their way. Her grandmother loved her and would light up when she visited her for the few more days she would be in town. A few days after she left, her grandmother died.

Exactly one month to her grandmother's stroke, Ashley got a stroke. Suffice it to say, it was difficult as she lost 50% of her eyesight. It turns out she had an AVM in her brain that we never knew she had.

Ashley remained in intensive care for three days to ensure the bleeding had stopped. After many tests of blood flow in her brain they released her. This young woman, the day after her release, forced me to take her to her University to start the reintegration process. In two weeks, she had already started taking a class even though it was clear she was tired, weak, and in pain. She ran her dad and mom ragged as we took turns taking care of her. She would not let that stroke deter her.

Ashley has since had the Cyber Knife procedure to radiate the offending ball of vessels with the expectation that they will dissipate. She is now making up the two-month rotation she missed in the winter with the expectation of staying close to her original schedule. I could not be a prouder dad as I watch her fight for her dream.

Supporters/subscribers/donors of Politics Done Right (Willies Media LLC) are the blood of this Activist Independent Progressive Media organization. We simply could not and cannot do it without you.

You frequently hear me say that Politics Done Right is yours. Make no mistake. That is not fake rhetoric, fake news, or an insincere statement. You are all an integral part of this endeavor and it is WE who are doing our part to nudge this country in the proper and humane direction. THANK YOU!

And of course, I will always be indebted to my fellow activists out there. The reality is that we all feed off each other's energy. We are never all in high spirits, so we take turns building each other up. More than ever we are going to have to keep propping each other up as this is a protracted battle for an egalitarian society that we are fighting for.

Chapter 9: About the Author

I received my Bachelor of Science in Mechanical Engineering from the University of Texas Austin. I have always been a political activist during and after college. After working in the oil business and for NASA companies as a senior software engineer/analyst/research engineer for five years, I decided to create my own software company, Willies Computer Software Co.

After doing business successfully for 20+ years, while I loved what I was doing, my passion has always been political activism. In fact, even as I ran my software company, I blogged politically under various pseudonyms.

Kingwood is a very conservative suburb and I did not want to out myself as a left-wing progressive for ill-effects it may have had on my daughter in school and during other activities. When she went off to college, I wound down my software company to work full time in political activism. It was the right time as our country is divided and tumultuous. I think I have the wherewithal to do my part to help heal the wounds and do my small part to help bring the country together.

I started the radio/media program Politics Done Right, the first program under my new company Willies Media LLC. It uses a voluntary funding method from our audience who see the importance of our work.

I was fortunate that KPFT 90.1 FM Houston was interested in Politics Done Right a few years after its inception. As such, we are able to fulfill part of our activist media actions. We do one day a week live on-air and five days a week over the internet (YouTube Live, Facebook Live, Periscope, Twitch, and every major podcast network)

Our goal is to discuss our political flashpoints from a Progressive point of view. We give people from every ideology the opportunity to have civil dialogue. We also interview local, national, and international political activists, politicians, and everyday citizens, ensuring everyone has a voice.

We intend to add other programs covering topics beyond politics but with humanity always at the forefront. We intend to add Spanish programming as well.

Chapter 10: Notes